VOCAL CONSISTENCY AND ARTISTIC FREEDOM

Existentialism and Vocal Instruction in Higher Education

by
Susan Boddie

VOCAL CONSISTENCY AND ARTISTIC FREEDOM

Existentialism and Vocal Instruction in Higher Education

by
Susan Boddie

COMMON GROUND RESEARCH NETWORKS 2021

First published in 2021
as part of *The Learner* Book Imprint
http://doi.org/doi:10.18848/978-1-86335-240-6/CGP (Full Book)

Common Ground Research Networks
60 Hazelwood Drive
University of Illinois Research Park
Champaign, IL
61820

Copyright © Susan Boddie 2021

All rights reserved. Apart from fair dealing for the purposes of study, research, criticism or review as permitted under the applicable copyright legislation, no part of this book may be reproduced by any process without written permission from the publisher.

Library of Congress Cataloging-in-Publication Data

Names: Boddie, Susan, author.
Title: Vocal consistency and artistic freedom : Existentialism and vocal instruction in higher education / Susan Boddie.
Description: Champaign : Common Ground Research Networks, 2021. | Includes bibliographical references and index. | Summary: "Many varying approaches to vocal instruction exist in higher education programs which appear to prolong inconsistency and unengaged performing. This research explores several existentialist principles of Jean-Paul Sartre and how these principles may inform and enhance current vocal teaching practice in higher education and perhaps better prepare new voice teachers. The study considers the effectiveness of the application of Sartre's existentialist principles and how they may inform vocal instruction and improve vocal development. In this way, this study is a pedagogical tool for currently practicing teachers as well as a valuable resource for new voice teachers"-- Provided by publisher.
Identifiers: LCCN 2021012813 (print) | LCCN 2021012814 (ebook) | ISBN 9780949313973 (hardback) | ISBN 9781863352390 (paperback) | ISBN 9781863352406 (adobe pdf)
Subjects: LCSH: Singing--Instruction and study. | Singing--Instruction and study--Philosophy. | Existentialism.
Classification: LCC MT820 .B66 2021 (print) | LCC MT820 (ebook) | DDC 783/.043071--dc23
LC record available at https://lccn.loc.gov/2021012813
LC ebook record available at https://lccn.loc.gov/2021012814

Cover Photo Credit: Phillip Kalantzis-Cope

Table of Contents

Chapter 1..1

The Challenge of Achieving a Consistent Resonant Singing Tone

Chapter 2..9

The National Schools of Singing

Chapter 3..63

Building the Student-Teacher Relationship

Chapter 4..95

Hermeneutic Phenomenology and Existentialism

Chapter 5..110

Freedom and Responsibility of the Singer

Chapter 6..135

Unlocking the Potential of Singers

References..137

DEDICATION

This study is dedicated to all musicians, and music instructors. To those that foster continued passion for the arts, and in particular to singers.

CHAPTER 1

The Challenge of Achieving a Consistent Resonant Singing Tone

As a vocal performance undergraduate student, I was frequently frustrated and discouraged by the inconsistent quality of my singing, since often I sounded like a different person in weekly lessons and daily practice. Meribeth Bunch Dayme (2005) states, "Aesthetically, the most important aspect of the voice is resonance, which comes mainly from the pharynx, a part of the vocal tract" (p. 68). It is disconcerting for a singer to not be able to achieve a consistent resonant singing tone. I remained unaware of how to mitigate this inconsistency until I pursued a master's degree and studied with renowned vocal pedagogue Patricia Misslin. Her approach, while somewhat holistic, was more of a natural approach. She attempted to instruct her students to sing independently. Jenny Dufault (2008) examined the teaching philosophy of my former teachersurveying the top percentage of metropolitan opera competition finalists and winners, researching and interviewing the three teachers who taught the majority of the winners. She observed that Misslin let the students find their own sound. She did not address tension or registers in the voice; instead, she used an approach of rhythm and movement and a positive learning environment in her lessons to help students discover their sound, and she focused on the feeling and experience of each voice. This is how Misslin instructed me while I studied at the Manhattan School of Music in New York City.

As I began my own teaching career and throughout many years of teaching, I utilized some of the ideas instilled in me by Misslin. However, I also explored the idea of instructing using an even more holistic singing approach that addresses the complete singer and views the student as an individual. The terms "holistic" and "wholistic" are often used interchangeably. For the purpose of this research study, the term "holistic" as it applies to education will be utilized. A holistic approach to education is one that aims to develop the emotional, spiritual, moral and psychological elements of the student, including the experience (Miller, 2007). In my daily teaching practice, I aid students in discovering their individual sound, breath support, and tension-free singing, striving to foster artistic performances by freeing students of the restrictions they often feel when unable to sing consistently. I attempt to instill responsibility and accountability in my students and expect them to take an active role in building technique and ownership of their voices.

There are parallels to Misslin's and my teaching approach to those of Jean-Paul Sartre's philosophical tenets that are central to existentialist thinking. As I began to explore existentialist principles, I was drawn in particular to Sartre and his ideas based in freedom and responsibility, and I considered to what extent they could be applied to vocal instruction. Sartre's principle of freedom offered a refreshing perspective in relation to the exploration of a teacher's freedom to become the type of teacher she[1] chooses utilizing a varied teaching skill set. the teacher's freedom to find her essence as a facilitator in the voice studio shifts this perspective from solely the technical components of what it means to sing. Freedom can be considered as student's free will and choice, and what she can become as a singer. Freedom is also one's artistic choices in performance. Freedom in singing is also about fundamentally tension-free singing. Sartre's principle of responsibility is the responsibility a voice teacher has as the facilitator in the student-teacher relationship and the ownership a student has in vocal study. The student is responsible for her outcome; the idea of "no excuses" according to Sartre (1984) is fundamental to using this teaching approach.

Sartre had an appreciation and love for music. It played an important role in his life, was part of his family, and remained throughout his life. His ideas on music and emotion in Situations (1965) resonated with me as a musician. He speaks of music, and freedom, and how music expresses and evokes emotion. It expresses the emotions of an age and may express the emotions of the oppressed or their hopes of a future. Sartre found solace, emotion, and freedom in music (Noudelmann, 2012). He played the piano daily, even later in his life when he lost his eyesight. Sartre (2001) includes the following statement:

> Sartre says of music it will always be over and above anything you can say about it. No matter how thorough the attempt to characterize in words what is expressed in music something remains uncaptured. Music says more than we can say that it says. (p. 289)

I was drawn to Sartre's appreciation of music as a musician; however, as I explored his central themes of freedom and responsibility and those ideas that stem from them (existence, essence, abandonment, and anguish), I thought it

---

[1] For this study, I have decided to use the generic third person "she" in most cases to balance the predominance of the masculine "he", "man," and "mankind" often found in the philosophical writings reviewed for this research study (Martyna, 1978, 1980; Sartre, 1984, 2007). This is a common practice for political philosophers (Brighouse & Swift, 2006; Swift, 2006).

would be beneficial to consider the ways in which Sartre's theory could inform voice teaching practice. This rationale will be further clarified in my theoretical framework.

The Inconsistency of Teaching Approaches

Inconsistent and emotionally unengaged singing by voice students is widespread, particularly in many university programs and in inexperienced singers. This was my experience as an undergraduate student, when I studied with many teachers who were not able to help me solve the problem of inconsistency. The source of the problem is perhaps a lack of voice teacher preparation as well as ambiguous approaches to vocal instruction in higher education. As I engaged in a preliminary literature review of vocal pedagogy degree programs and philosophies of vocal instruction to frame the discussion of inconsistent and unemotional singing, I discovered there are many different teaching approaches that may further such inconsistencies. These will be discussed in more detail in my literature review.

Many students I have observed on voice jury panels, in lessons, performances, recitals and competitions exhibit technical deficiencies and inconsistencies such as poor posture, lack of consistent breath support, the inability to balance resonance throughout their vocal range, a habit of pushing the voice, and unemotional performances. Smith and Chipman (2007) write, "It is common for singers to 'phone in' performances not 'being in the moment' of their performance or creating something fresh and new" (p. 23). Emotions generated by the performer and audience members in a performing art such as singing are created in the present at the moment it is being created as opposed to other creative arts such as writing or painting. The reaction to these other art forms is generated after their creation. This immediacy of creation is why it is so essential for a singer to be emotionally engaged in performance. They further explain that "because singing must be constantly created in the moment, we must have a technique for it that moves through time as well" (p. 23). At the time of performance, the singer must explore her artistic freedom and not focus on, or be distracted by, technique. Technical deficiencies will prolong the inability to emotionally connect to music. Joan Patenaude-Yarnell (2004) also notes the technical deficiencies and adds that many students also display the inability to sing *fioratura*[2] and lack the ability to sing *legato*.[3]

A study examining the vocal mechanics of untrained singers (an untrained singer in the study is a student with fewer than two years of training) identifies

---

[2] Florid, fast phrases of music.
[3] Smooth, sustained music passages.

complaints and inconsistencies in technique from students. Complaints such as hoarseness, breathiness in tone (lack of resonance or ring in the sound), laryngeal tension, and decreased range are identified as predominant problems for inexperienced singers. Teachey, Kahane and Beckford (1991) discuss how "lacking sufficient formal vocal training, the untrained or minimally trained singer has a poor understanding of the capacities and limitations of the vocal mechanism" (p. 55). The researchers find a high incidence of vocal lesions in inexperienced singers. Inconsistent singing or misuse can lead to fatigue and other more serious issues. Tammy Frederick observes that "the number one cause of hoarseness and vocal fatigue is poor vocal technique" (2006, p. 32). A singer who does not have an awareness of how his or her voice functions has poor technique. This causes the singer to try to force a sound from the vocal folds without engaging any of the resonators in the body designed for amplifying the voice such as the neck, skull, sinuses, chest, and vocal tract. Frederick explains further: "If you find you get hoarse after performing or rehearsing it is very likely that you are singing with a high larynx. To make matters worse, you are probably forcing large amounts of air through this high larynx by shouting or singing loudly" (p. 32). When this occurs, one has tension in the throat and fatigue will set in. Many of these common vocal complaints and inconsistencies have been identified by researchers (Sataloff, 1998). An individual singing without technical consistency will experience a great deal of fatigue or swelling in the vocal folds.

Some higher education vocal pedagogy programs have teaching practicum courses,[4] in which a student teaches another student and is supervised; however, there appear to be no courses or parts of voice pedagogy textbooks that address the relationship of the teacher and student and the important consequences of how a student is taught (Alderson, 1979; Bunch, 1997, 2005; Deere, 2005; Doscher, 1994; Hines, 1982; McKinney, 2005; Miller,1986, Sataloff, 1998; Vennard, 1967; Ware, 1998; Whitlock, 1975). Not addressing these important consequences can further inconsistent and unengaged singing, as teachers will not know how to relay information to students. It is not indicated how much supervision and mentoring takes place in these programs.[5] In examining voice pedagogy classes at her institute, Patti

---

[4] Reviews of graduate vocal pedagogy programs show that while some institutions have minimal pedagogy courses that are part of degree programs, their focus remaining on the performance aspect. Some students have limited teaching practicum supervision. Course content is based in vocal science, history, and vocal performance.

[5] A number of universities offer vocal pedagogy programs, including: Kansas University, Manhattan School of Music, McGill University, New England Conservatory, Ohio State University, Shenandoah University, University of Colorado, University of Miami, University of North Carolina, University of North Texas, University of Texas, University of Toronto, and Westminster Choir College.

Peterson (2004) realized that supervision and mentoring of voice students is actually quite limited. Graduate students may receive mentoring for just several days per term and the hope is that the void in guidance will be filled by one or two basic pedagogy courses. This may further the problem of inconsistent singing. Not only are pedagogy programs focusing on the science of singing, it appears that there is limited mentoring and supervision of pre-service teachers.[6] It is important to understand the anatomy of the voice, the breath mechanism, phonation, and articulation in order to learn and instruct the technique of singing; however, this does not help the student obtain consistent vocal technique if the teacher-student relationship does not translate this information holistically.

This is an educational problem. It is my intention to explore the relationship of the teacher and student – it is central to help the student find vocal consistency and artistic freedom. More specifically, the higher education problem this study offers ways to consider makes recommendations for vocal instruction. Addressing the student-teacher relationship in the voice studio and applying existentialist principles such as freedom and responsibility may result in a relationship that aids consistent and emotionally engaged singing in higher education. In so doing, this study may encourage better curriculum design in vocal pedagogy programs as well as more self-awareness in current voice practitioners. A student who is instructed by a teacher with a varied skill set may become aware of her freedom. In so doing the teacher also the opportunity to explore her own freedom to become the type of instructor she wishes to be.

Many current vocal pedagogy degree programs, textbooks, and research projects are lacking the important element of the teacher-student relationship with the teacher as facilitator. Pamela Wurgler (1997) poses the question:

> Why do most fledging voice teachers spend their first few years of teaching "reinventing the wheel?" Why do most teach as they were taught, not as they were taught to teach? It is possible that they were not taught how to teach? (p. 3)

These contrasting views on instructing singers emphasize just one aspect of the singer and appear ambiguous and underdeveloped. They do not take the entire singer into consideration and, thus, may contribute to the problem of inconsistency. Existentialism offers an interesting way to reconceptualise the view of vocal instruction and may result in more consistent and emotional

---

[6] Pre-service teachers for the purpose of this study are music students in vocal pedagogy degree programs who have not taught outside their academic institutions. Graduates are those who instruct in higher education institutions or private voice studios.

singing. For this reason, part of the research will also attend to re-engaging students' experience of joy in singing, as well as keeping this important live art form relevant in a culture where so much is manufactured and created artificially. A teacher can guide this passion, encourage, and motivate the student.

The role of Sartre's existentialist principles of freedom and responsibility for the singer. This study draws upon Jean-Paul Sartre's central existentialist principles of freedom and responsibility, and upon those that stem from them: namely existence, essence, responsibility, and freedom (facticity, abandonment, and anguish). It discusses these as they apply to and may inform and enhance current vocal pedagogy practice, specifically in fostering consistent and emotionally engaged singing in voice students. These terms will be defined in more detail in the overview of Sartre's existentialism later in this paper. Sartre states (1993), "Existentialism's first move is to make every man aware of what he is and to make the full responsibility of his existence rest on him" (p. 36). This statement exemplifies the research. This research study will examine a pedagogical method of vocal instruction informed by Sartre's existentialist principles of freedom and responsibility in order to consider the extent to which it facilitates[7] consistent and engaged singing. This research has potential impact upon vocal instruction at the higher education level and in vocal pedagogy degree programs. While I will include a review of other existential educational researchers, the primary influence of the study is Sartre and his central tenets of freedom and responsibility.

Consideration of Jean-Paul Sartre's Existentialist Philosophy

This study considers the application of vocal instruction at the higher education level by drawing upon existentialist principles in order to facilitate consistent and emotionally engaged singing. Specifically, in drawing upon the principles of existentialism, my aim is to refocus current vocal pedagogical practices by taking into consideration the relationship of the teacher and student, with the teacher as a facilitator in vocal study. The central guiding principle of a teaching method influenced by existentialism is to view the student as an individual, instructing and guiding him or her to be responsible

---

[7] For the purpose of this study in vocal instruction, the terms facilitate, and facilitator is used as a way to describe an instructor that effectively guides the voice student individually to make discoveries in a humanistic student-teacher relationship. This is in contrast to the term teacher which I define for this study as one who may not address the individual needs of the voice student. Facilitators of vocal instruction make students responsible for their own learning and discoveries. In contrast, the teacher in this study may possess knowledge or information but is perhaps not able to guide the student to her own discoveries (Sunnarborg, 2013).

for learning while helping the student to find individual freedom. Thus, the central question for consideration by students and teachers is:

> To what extent can Jean-Paul Sartre's existentialist principles of responsibility and freedom suitably influence the student-teacher relationship and be applied to vocal development to improve inconsistent and emotionally unengaged singing in undergraduate music students?

Significance of the Study

The study is significant and may be helpful to those in the field of vocal instruction and vocal pedagogy degree programs. Many teaching philosophies currently used in higher education institutions appear to have significant ambiguity. The study reviewed several of these philosophies and explored the use of a varied set of teaching tools that may help foster consistent and emotionally engaged performances in students studying voice and may help them gain responsibility in the learning process as well as find freedom in performance and expression. These tenets studied are for consideration by teachers currently instructing in higher education. As well, the study may offer students in vocal pedagogy degree programs an approach to consider when they begin to instruct voice.

The application of the existentialist principles of Jean-Paul Sartre and other existentialist philosophers has been considered in relation to general education, and the use of arts in the classroom. A method of piano instruction at the higher education level that uses existentialist principles has already been explored (Mortyakova, 2009); however, there has been no significant research in vocal instruction and the influence of existentialist principles. This study presents the field of the philosophy of education and vocal instruction with new research that may prompt discussion and debate in pedagogical approaches to vocal instruction. This debate may result in a refocus or may encourage current vocal instructors to reflect on their methodologies. This can be beneficial to students. An instructor who is willing to reflect and to explore his or her own freedom in how he or she instructs consequently may help students engaged in vocal study explore their freedom and reach a higher level of performance.

The problem of inconsistent and emotionally unengaged singing has been identified. This study acts as an attempt to offer ways to help mitigate this problem, which stems from teaching. In order to understand how this problem originates as a teaching problem, it is important to explore various methods of vocal instruction in order to examine where there are inconsistencies in tenets as well as much ambiguity. The history of many of the teaching methods used in higher education music programs stems from European national schools of singing. In the next chapter, the national schools of singing will be described as well as examples of some current methods of vocal instruction used in higher education.

CHAPTER 2

The National Schools of Singing

In order to understand approaches to vocal instruction, one must consider the precursor to methods used in higher education institutions. The educational background a vocal pedagogue obtains can be a blend of cultural influence in teaching and tradition and the technical approach instructed by her teacher or teachers. The pedagogue's teacher may have had various influences on his or her pedagogical approach as well. In the field of vocal instruction, teachers pass on information to their students based on what they experienced as students and performers themselves, as well as the technical approach or blend of approaches they learned throughout their careers. Given that teachers commonly teach as they were instructed, it is important to first consider the dominant approaches, or "national schools of singing" that have informed vocal instruction. The national schools of singing (Italian, English, German, and French) have influenced the varied approaches used in higher education in North America today. These schools will be described in this chapter. Following this description, several overarching categories of teaching practice will be examined.

It is important to understand some of the historic approaches to teaching in order to recognize their influence on current teaching practices at higher education institutions. Deere (2002) indicates, "A teacher's knowledge of the styles and approaches in teaching singing can help identify the tradition from which the teacher has evolved" (p. 8). There are several western European countries that exhibit national tendencies and a distinct approach to certain aspects of the study of vocal technique. There are also some commonalities, and these will be discussed in further detail in this portion of this section. Western European schools of thought have influenced how voice is taught in institutions in North America, as much of the repertoire that is studied in classical voice programs originates from Europe. Richard Miller (1977) engaged in a study examining the vocal techniques of several western European schools of thought to compare historic ideas as well as tendencies that were current when the first edition of his book was published in 1977. Since this publication, there have been changes in teaching practice, such as more attention to the science and physiology of singing, vocal health, and the use of technology in the voice studio. For this reason, Miller (1977) thought it appropriate to re-examine the national schools to see if tendencies remained or changed with time. He found that little had changed in the fundamental tenets of vocal instruction he had studied years before. He did discover, however, that students, upon graduation from higher education institutions in their native countries, have increased mobility as they engage in professional performing careers. This mobility requires that singers modify their techniques for a more standardized international approach to singing for performance purposes, in order to appeal to a broad audience. As well, he notes there are more technical demands placed on performers as concert halls increase in size, and as performances are scheduled close together, often requiring the performer to travel a great deal. A performer also faces the challenge of the rehearsal demands of a stage manager or of an orchestral conductor who is often not a singer. This can put considerable strain on her instrument and technique. Additionally, new demands are put on singers by contemporary composers as they write vocal music that is more technically demanding for the singer in terms of vocal range, dynamic contrast, or manipulation of the vocal sound than the *bel canto*[8] era of vocal literature (Miller, 1997). Other researchers have studied the national schools and their tenets (Blankenbehler, 2009; Cobb-Jordan, 2001; Elliott, 2007; Fields, 1970; Holland, 2008; Lehmann, 1993; Monahan, 1978; Sanford, 1995; Sell, 2005; Stark, 1999; Wakefield, 2003).

    The national schools that have influenced performance practice and the instruction of vocal technique in North America are the German, Italian, French, and English schools of thought (Blankenbehler, 2009; Cobb-Jordan, 2001; Elliott, 2007; Holland, 2008; Lehmann, 1993; Miller, 1977, 1997; Sell, 2005; Stark, 1999).

    I will present an overview of the pedagogical tenets for the soprano, mezzo/contralto, tenor, baritone, and bass voice in each national school of thought. There are similar as well as distinguishing characteristics between the four schools. As I will begin with the soprano voice, this section will contain the most in-depth explanation, in order to avoid repetition in the sections that follow. The pedagogical approach to vocal instruction is quite similar for the soprano, mezzo, contralto, tenor, and baritone voices in the respective national schools. I will discuss some of the potentially positive and negative aspects of each national school. Many of the schools borrowed characteristics from each other, so parallels will be noted as well as differences. This background is relevant in identifying which schools have influenced how certain aspects of vocal instruction are approached in higher education institutions today.

---

[8] *Bel canto* is defined as beautiful singing. This is characterized by an ability to sing a legato or smooth vocal line effortlessly or beautifully, as well the ability to sing *fioritura,* or rapid, florid passages of music.

THE SOPRANO VOICE

The soprano voice is the highest female vocal category. The soprano voice can be classified as *coloratura* (a voice that has extreme agility, a vast range, and is either a medium or full voice), *soubrette* (very light), *lyric* (can be light or full) or *dramatic* (large, full voice, often without agility). The method of vocal instruction for the soprano voice in the German, Italian, French, and finally English traditions will now be described.

The German approach to instructing vocal tone (resonance or timbre) for the coloratura consists of removing a great deal of *vibrato* (natural vibration of the vocal folds) from the sound in both *legato* (smooth) and agile music passages. Minimizing vibrato quality is achieved with an open, vertical mouth position. This position pulls down the palate and removes the resonant, ringing tone from the sound. The soubrette voice is instructed in a similar manner, removing a great deal of natural vibrato or vibrancy in the sound. The soubrette character role in opera often requires charm and a coquettish nature. The German school does encourage a small amount of vibrancy in the sound as a way to depict this character, but much less so than other national schools. The German lyric soprano is trained to maintain some vibrato in her tone; however, the desired tone is covered or dampened and lacking the brilliance that will be described in her Italian counterpart. The dramatic soprano is instructed in the same manner as other German sopranos: the sound is round, darkened, or covered (Miller, 1986, 1996, 2004). If one imagines a Wagnerian soprano sustaining a high note with a great deal of power and a dark tone that lacks much vibrato, this accurately describes the typical German sound. Singing without vibrato causes tension in the vocal fold region (Bunch Dayme, 2005). As well, attempting to darken one's natural tone can result in intonation issues (singing flat), as well as tension in the throat and a tone that does not have a ringing quality. A tone without a ringing quality will not resonate in a frequency that projects a great distance in a larger space.

Students from the German tradition are trained with abundant imagery to facilitate singing in this manner (Miller, 1977, 1997; Stark 1999). Imagery is still used by some voice teachers in institutions today. This will be explored in greater detail in the pedagogical methods analysis portion of this study. German students are instructed to widen the throat, or to think of placing or imagining the voice at the back of the throat depressing the tongue. Lehmann (1993), in her book originally titled *Meine Gesangskunst*, speaks of flattening the tongue, depressing it as if to create a furrow in the tongue (p. 111). Students are instructed to imagine that there is an orange or other type of round food in the back of the throat in order to open the throat. Students are also instructed to imagine their tone as "up and over." This means that the singer must imagine her sound first focused at the back of her throat and then moving through the crown of her head (Cobb-Jordan, 2001; Holland, 2008;

Lehmann, 1993; Miller, 1977, 1997; Sell, 2005). This approach requires imagery, control, and holding of the vocal mechanism. I believe that a tone should be directed in a forward manner, in order to project in the direction of the audience. A student who imagines aiming her tone to the back of the throat, before thinking of the tone as forward, will risk trapping the tone in the back of her throat. A tone that is trapped in the back of the throat can become tense and under pitch, and it may not project very far.

It is important to note the German approach to breath and voice registration (chest, middle, head, and flute). As in some other schools, the idea of breath support in the German school for all voice types requires a low abdominal breath; however, this is primarily focused in the back and extreme lower abdomen, which the singer must distend. German singers are instructed to keep the sternum low—almost compressed—as a way to prohibit air from entering the upper area of the lungs and thus keeping all support low. Breath support for the German singer comes from maintaining fullness in the abdomen, and from contracting and rotating the pelvis and buttock area as a way to support the sound. Singers are encouraged to maintain tension in the lower region of the body and to push out the abdomen while holding firmness in the body (Blades-Zeller, 2003; Cobb-Jordan, 2001; Holland, 2008; Lehmann, 1993; Miller 1977, 1997; Stark, 1999). There is a great deal of holding in the body in the German school of singing (Miller, 1977, 1997; Stark 1999). Lehmann (1993) writes, "A singer can become and continue to be master of his voice and means of expression only as long as he practices daily conscious vocal gymnastics" (p. 132) and also that "the first thing needed is to bring the body under control" (p. 263). This is in direct contrast to further-illustrated schools of thought that encourage a cycle of tension-free air flow without holding the body. There is concern when terms such as hold, control, push, and contract are used in relation to singing. Tension or constriction in one's body will cause one's sound to exhibit these same characteristics. For a singer, the body is the instrument. If there is tension, constriction, holding, or forcing in an approach to singing, this can translate to a sound that is tense and constricted, not free-flowing or effortless.

The principles of vocal registration and resonance in the German school also differ from other pedagogical traditions. It is believed that in order to build range and volume, the singer must completely separate each register of her voice, particularly the lower chest and upper head register, and work on each area independently. This is called *Stimmbildung* or "formation of the voice." This technique is taught to both female and male students. The voice is taken apart and then rebuilt. Often German female singers are instructed to maintain a light, airy sound even while singing in the lower register. The German school does not encourage what is referred to as *open chest* (a sound produced as a female speaks in a low speaking voice with vibration in the sternum). Lehmann (1993) considered a great deal of head voice in the singing tone the secret to maintaining a youthful voice and believed that it would preserve the voice while singing heavy repertoire.

This approach can inhibit a full sound, particularly for music written in a low range, and may result in a thin sound. Miller (1997) writes of the German school of thought: "Frequently is it maintained that the voice must first be taken apart, the component parts developed and then re-assembled" (p. 67). This methodology is a compartmentalised approach to instruction. Other methods in institutions that focus on just one aspect of the singer will be explored further in this paper.

Another pedagogical approach in the German tradition is the use of the *Kopfstimme*. This is a particular sound unique to the German tradition of singing. *Kopfstimme* resembles a light, hovering head tone voice quality with a great deal of breath allowed to enter the sound. Vocal resonance is imaged in the back of the throat, with little vibrancy or vibrato. The tone can be a pleasant tone. If one listens to singers such as soprano Elizabeth Schwarzkopf or baritone Dietrich Fischer-Dieskau, one will experience examples of *Kopfstimme*. These were, however, highly trained singers. If an inexperienced student attempts to allow a great deal of breath to enter his or her tone as well as aiming the voice to the back of the throat, the resulting sound can be tense, breathy, and under pitch. This is not a desirable tonal quality to emit.

In contrast, the Italian approach to teaching vocal tone or resonance in the soprano voice is quite different from the German school (Blades-Zeller, 2003; Clements, 2008; Miller, 1977, 1986; 1997; Sell, 2005; Stark, 1999). The desired sound is vibrant throughout the full range of the singer. The coloratura approaches rapid passages of music with a great deal of vibrato and a bright tone. This is achieved by lifting the *mask* (the cheekbones), which in turn lifts the palate and combines with exposing the upper teeth for a somewhat horizontal mouth position (Cobb-Jordan, 2001; Lamperti, 1890; Marchesi, 1970; Miller, 1997). This may produce shrillness in the sound if not approached moderately. The sound is placed forward, but not as forward as in the French tradition of singing I later describe. The light soubrette voice is also trained to sing with brilliance, with a great deal of lift in the palate and exposure of the front teeth. The Italian lyric soprano tone and approach to teaching is often considered an ideal sound and approach. The teaching methodology for this voice encourages brilliance, warmth, and vibrancy in the tone. This is achieved in the same manner as for the soubrette or coloratura singer. Potential shrillness is balanced by the heavier weight of this voice type. The large lyric voice or *spinto* is also trained to sing with brilliance, in direct opposition to her German colleague who is instructed to cover and dampen her tone. The large sound of the dramatic soprano is also encouraged, in order to use brilliance, vibrato, and a great deal of lift or smile in her approach to singing.

The Italian approach to breath for all voice types represents well-balanced muscle coordination. This approach to singing is called *appoggio* [9] (Blankenbehler, 2009; Cobb-Jordan, 2001; Marchesi, 1970; Monahan, 1978; Miller, 1986, 1997, 2004; Stark, 1999). The breath is taken in low, as in the German school: however, there is no holding or restriction. The sternum is not pulled down nor compressed. It is suspended in a poised position and it remains this way. There is little movement in the sternum; it is not held but, rather maintained while singing. Breath is taken in with a relaxed, open throat. The Italian student is trained to achieve full expansion in the back, sides, and abdomen, releasing the intercostal muscles in order to obtain a great deal of air at inhalation. While maintaining the ribs in an open position with the sternum suspended, the singer pulls the abdominal wall in to release the air, thus creating support without holding or causing tension in other parts of the body. The body remains strong, is not held, and does not collapse. It is a steady and consistent cycle in and out of the breath.

The Italian approach to registration for all voice types is a balanced blend of what is considered the open chest, the lower middle, the upper middle, the upper register, and the bell or flute tones. The Italian singer is trained to balance and blend her voice while moving through each passage of her voice. Unlike the training in the German or English school, which will be described, all registers are used with an even mixture of what is considered chest, middle, and head voice, although the mechanics of singing all take place in the larynx, pharynx, and vocal folds.

The Italian approach to instructing breath, tone, and registration represents a well-balanced approach. It is a method that attempts to use the full range and capacity of the sound of the singer. As well, the approach strives for tension-free singing. This is a desirable and healthy approach to use in vocal instruction for students. It encourages support, not tension of the sound, and finds the maximum amount of resonance that the body can produce.

The French method of instructing sopranos has some parallels to the Italian school, in that the desired tone is a beautiful tone; however, it achieved from a very natural approach to singing (Cobb-Jordan, 2001; Miller, 1977, 1997; Reid, 1972; Sell, 2005). This natural approach to instruction is used in some higher education institutions today. This will be explained in further detail in the pedagogical method analysis section of this research study.

The French pedagogical approach to instruction is a very relaxed and perhaps unstructured approach to technique and to music interpretation, very much in contrast to the German school. Bernac writes (1970), "the aim is to

---

[9] *Appoggio* is a term to describe the Italian method of muscle and breath coordination that results in a balanced, smooth, and pleasant vocal tone, i.e. the bel canto tone.

give aesthetic pleasure through pure music, stripped of all philosophical, literary, or humanistic significance, such as that which goes so willingly hand in hand with German music" (p. 33). The approach is quite natural, though some pedagogues believe it too natural and lacking energy (Cobb-Jordan, 2001; Holland, 2008; Miller, 1977, 1997). The French pedagogues were known for "their belief in natural breathing and laryngeal freedom" (Holland, 2008, p. 7). Much of the focus in the French method is "concerned with sensitive perceptions and impressions" (Bernac, 1970, p. 34).

The French method of instructing the coloratura soprano is somewhat similar to that of the Italian approach. The desired sound or voice placement is extremely forward—more forward than the Italian school—as it is placed far forward in the mask. The result can be described at times as a "white noise" tone quality, lacking warmth (Monahan, 1978). The French tone may also be considered somewhat nasal in timbre, even when not singing required French nasal vowels (Miller 1977, 1997). Miller (1997) also notes that many French teachers and singers find the bell or flute tones quite pleasing, and that sopranos tend to vocalise a great deal in this register with less balancing through the registers than the Italian singer exhibits.

The French soubrette soprano is instructed to maintain brilliance in her tone, but also to maintain a very lightly weighted tone. This tone, without a great deal of power or weight, is a result of an unenergetic or natural breath support and a relaxed approach to singing. "The French objective was for a natural tone and beauty in singing with no physical limitations or strains on the body and voice" (Cobb-Jordan, 2001, p. 9). It desirable to not induce strain on the body or voice; nonetheless, one must use an energized approach to singing classical repertoire, and it is not a natural activity. The French lyric soprano is also trained to place her sound forward, somewhat similar to her Italian counterpart's placement, while maintaining brilliance. There is, however, less vibrancy or substance to the sound of French singers than to those of other countries, due to the natural approach to breath support. Perhaps there is less body involvement in supporting the voice, so one is only able to experience a superficial level of tonal quality and volume (Miller, 1997; Sanford, 1995). Miller (1997) tells the reader that it is uncommon to find a full lyric or dramatic voice in the French tradition, perhaps due to an approach to teaching breath support that lacks energy and physical involvement in supporting sound.

Breath technique in the French school is instructed as natural breathing. Students are instructed to use the same breath they use in speaking for the singing voice. French students are to maintain a relaxed posture, but are often given little more instruction (Sanford, 1995). In the French approach, "teachers of this method suggest the student not think about breathing" (Cobb-Jordan, 2001, p. 9). This produces a singing tone that lacks energy and may explain why a lack of vibrant, brilliant voices or voices with dynamic volume appears to exist in the French tradition of singing.

The English school strives to achieve a unique approach to pedagogy and sound that is not influenced by the German and Italian traditions. Choral music had a significant impact historically on how voice was instructed in England (Miller, 1977, 1997; Stark, 1999). The English unchanged male soprano choral tone is a straight tone—sharp and perhaps without warmth. This tone impacts adult singing as well, particularly in the choral setting. The English national school trains singers to obtain a pure tone, as one might expect for sacred choral music.

The English coloratura soprano student is instructed to produce a tone that resembles a flute, quite similar to the German methodology in that the desired tone is pure and without much vibrato or color, lacking the brilliance one would hear in an Italian or perhaps a French singer. The soubrette also resembles the coloratura with, however, more vibrancy. The soubrette character in opera generally exhibits more of a coquettish nature than the coloratura or lyric soprano roles. In the English tradition of teaching, there are two distinct methods to instructing lyric sopranos. The first method is to sing music—particularly sacred music—much like the unchanged male soprano previously described, with flute-like, sharp tones lacking vibrato. A distinctly English approach still exists in which singers are trained to retain a pure tone without color or vibrato. This tone is not "pure" according to the physiology of singing. The vocal folds naturally vibrate when air flows across them, such as when one plucks a guitar or violin string, and energy is transferred through the string and vibrates, creating a natural wave with overtones (Bunch, 1997). In this aspect, it is quite similar to the German teaching tradition of controlling the voice while holding tension in the breath. The second approach to instructing the lyric soprano parallels an Italian sound in tone production but not in breath support. The dramatic soprano strives for an Italian quality by keeping vibrancy and fullness in the sound, but lacks the breath support training to sustain this sound.

The English approach to teaching registration and resonance is similar to the German pedagogy in that the voice is to be focused on the back of the throat and then directed towards the crown, while removing much of the vibrato from the sound. The tone is described as a *cathedral tone* (Cobb-Jordan, 2001; Fields, 1970; Holland, 2008; Miller, 1977, 1997; Sell, 2005; Stark, 1999). This tone is without vibrato, a "white noise" tone effect that resembles an unchanged boy soprano tonal quality. As indicated, there are two schools of thought when instructing the lyric soprano: one promotes the cathedral tone and the other a more Italian- influenced approach to instructing to the navigation of registers and tone. The English tradition is similar to the German teaching approach with regard to the lack of mixing in registers. Instructors who teach the cathedral tone encourage a great deal of head register and little chest or open chest. Singers who are instructed in an Italian influenced pedagogy attempt blending and balance between registers, although much less so than in the bel canto tradition.

The breath approach instructed in the English tradition of singing is unique. One is to take in air quite high in the back and sternum. It is common to see English singers inhale with lifted shoulders, leaning slightly forward. It is very different from the lower abdominal breath technique one finds in the German and Italian method. Shakespeare (1910) writes, "For singing purposes, diaphragmatic breathing must be combined with upper rib breathing" (p. 9).

Using an approach based in the English cathedral tone tradition appears to have a similar tonal quality to the French style of singing, although perhaps lacking some of the nasality in the tone. Attempting to create a vocal tone without color, resonance, or vibrato will cause tension in the throat. Holding or constricting the vocal mechanism is not a healthy approach to singing, as I previously mentioned. Perhaps instructors are motivated to use this tone so as not to hear an individual sound in a group of singers, an effect which may be desirable for a choral conductor. It is, however, possibly detrimental to the singer. As well, taking breath high in the body while lifting the shoulders, causes tension in the sternum, neck, and shoulder area and, in turn, affects the natural functioning of the vocal mechanism and tension in the vocal folds.

The next section explores the approaches used in various national traditions to instruct the mezzo soprano and contralto voice. There will be tenets similar to those used in instructing the soprano voice.

MEZZO-SOPRANO AND CONTRALTO VOICES

The previously described technical aspects of the German School for instructing the soprano are quite similar to the pedagogical approach used when training the heavier mezzo and contralto female voices. One also finds the categories of coloratura, lyric voices of varying sizes, and the dramatic voice in this category of female singer. The German singer with a voice that sits in the lower mezzo range is encouraged to drop the larynx, pull back the tongue, and open the throat. As was indicated in the preceding section, many German singers are given the image of an orange, or other large object sitting at the back of the throat (Cobb-Jordan, 2001; Miller, 1977, 1997). The lack of open chest resonance or blending of registers is still expected for this type of singer. One must consider the challenge for a singer instructed to sing repertoire set in a lower register while attempting to maintain a lighter voice quality. The resulting sound will resemble two singers, as there will be a large break between her vocal registers. With such an importance placed on emotion in German music, it would seem difficult for a singer to express emotion in her lower register while using a lighter tone.

The Italian tradition of pedagogy for the mezzo and contralto parallels the tenets taught to her soprano counterpart. The singer is instructed to maintain a bel canto, smooth, agile, unforced sounds with balanced *appoggio*. The Italian singers of the mezzo and contralto categories are instructed as is the soprano to balance registers and place the sound forward for brilliance in the tone. Miller indicates (1997), "Her dramatically powerful top voice and exciting focus of sound distinguish her from the kinds of timbre preferences which pertain among mezzos in other schools" (p. 151). The Italian tradition of instruction with the soprano voice encourages a healthy, balanced approach to singing.

The French tradition of instructing the mezzo or contralto, according to Miller (1997), is the result of encountering a soprano who has insufficient range, breath support, and brilliance to perform challenging soprano repertoire. The mezzo and contralto singers are instructed to sing as the French soprano in this pedagogical tradition with a light, natural tone that is placed far forward in the mask. The breath support for singing "should be as if asleep" (Cobb-Jordan, 2001, p. 9). Heavier repertoire, such that a dramatic singer should navigate with ease, encompassing sustained phrases, drastic dynamic change, and broad vocal range, presents a challenge to the singer who does not have strong breath support or muscle coordination, as "body and voice simply do not get together to a sufficient degree to accomplish the proper negotiation of upper voice" (Miller, 1997, p. 154). The French tradition of singing does not appear to work well with the mezzo or contralto ranges, particularly due to a trend for maintaining a lighter singing tone.

The mezzo or contralto instructed in the English school of thought "is generally incapable of negotiating either the mezzo-coloratura or the dramatic mezzo literatures with any degree of skill" (Miller, 1997, p. 152). This voice category is instructed, as is the soprano, to breathe high in the torso and upper back and, as other singers in this tradition, to drop the jaw. This can result in poor diction. As well as negatively impacting diction, dropping the jaw, as in the German tradition, will pull down the palate and force the sound back in the throat causing the tone to lose brilliance and vibrancy.

The approach to instructing the mezzo and contralto voice in western European traditions, with perhaps the exception of the Italian school, appears to present challenges for some singers when they attempt to sing certain genres of repertoire. However, it may be well received by the national audiences of each respective country, who are accustomed to hearing native singers.

The next section explores the European traditions for instructing the male voices: tenor and bass/baritone. The teaching method is quite similar to the approach used in instructing the female voices.

THE TENOR VOICE

The male voices in the western European schools of pedagogical thought are instructed on technical aspects of singing such as breath, resonance, and registration much as are their female counterparts, while addressing the male gender's unique voice registration category, the male falsetto (Cobb-Jordan, 2001; Miller, 1977, 1997, 2004; Sell, 2005; Stark, 1999).

The light German tenor is not instructed to use the traditional covered, heavy sound found in other male and female voices in this pedagogical school of thought. He is instructed, as is the female student, to use little vibrato but to try to incorporate some brilliance, while still being obliged to think of the voice staying at the back of the throat. This presents a challenge for the singer, who is resonating tone at the back of the throat but is somehow supposed to strive for brilliance. Similar to this light tenor is the comic tenor, who also possesses a light voice and is instructed in much the same manner. The light and comic tenors are both instructed using a great deal of imagery similar to that employed when instructing female singers. The light and comic tenors tend to imagine the voice staying in the back of the throat. The light tenor is instructed to use the *Kopfstimme* (floating) tone. This tone is frequently heard in early baroque music and in the category of a Bach tenor. Similar to the tone heard in the English tradition, it has very little vibrato. The lyric tenor with a heavier tone, also known as the *Heldentenor*, is instructed to use a more traditional German approach to singing. This approach incorporates the technique that has been previously described with dampening and covering, as well as low breathing with a pelvic tilt and tension in the abdomen and lower body. The method of singing may cause tension in the vocal folds as well as potentially inhibit a circular motion of breath.

In contrast to the German pedagogical approach to singing, the Italian follows the same tradition for instructing tenors as it does with its female singers. The desired tone is a brilliant, vibrant tone achieved with a relaxed throat and a lifted palate for optimal resonance combined with breath coordination. The light tenor with less vocal power than other genres of tenor is instructed with the Italian approach of *appoggio* (coordination of breath, resonance and registration), although he is often instructed not to attempt to give too much breath in his upper voice, as he does not possess the ability to open his sound as does his lyric or dramatic tenor colleague. The lyric tenor is considered as is the soprano to have the ability to balance breath, resonance, and registration. He must be able to use his full sound with a blend of chest, middle, and head voice with the ability to be expressive with his instrument. The spinto or large lyric voice is instructed as are the large female voices, to maintain a great deal of brilliance with breath support without tension or holding. The tone should be "free-flowing and unimpeded" (Miller, 1997, p.

156). This is in contrast to the German tradition, in which one finds a great deal of control and tension in the breath.

The French approach to the instruction of tenor singing is quite similar to the methodology used when instructing female singers. The goal is the most natural approach to breathing. That is, breathing should be without effort, and should have a great deal of focus on putting the voice primarily in the nasal passages. Italian bel canto singer and teacher Enrico Caruso (1975) writes, "Many teachers, especially the French, make a point of placing the voice in the nasal cavity on the pretext of strengthening it" (p. 57). He is quite critical of the French tradition of placing the voice into the mask and says further, "the 'bleat' or goat voice, a particular fault of French singers, proceeds from the habit of forcing the voice, which, when it is of small volume, cannot stand the consequent fatigue of the larynx" (p. 58). The majority of French tenor voices appear to be light; perhaps this is due to an approach to breath support that parallels what one would use while at rest, resulting in a tone with little weight. The majority of French tenor voices, according to Miller (1997), are light tenors with a small range and "a short top voice, the result of the hesitancy on the part of the French school to fully utilize muscular antagonism and sub glottal pressure during the act of singing much beyond the requirements of speech" (p. 154). There appears to be a limited number of French tenors with large lyric, spinto, or dramatic characteristics: "potential tenor voices of any weight in France are generally considered to be lyric baritones and are handled accordingly" (p. 154).

The pedagogical approach to instructing tenor voices in the French tradition parallels the approach taken when instructing female voices. The natural approach to breath and use of primarily nasal resonance without incorporating all resonating chambers available to a singer (mouth, pharynx, nasal, and head cavities) contributes to the lighter quality of singing observed in the French tradition. This approach may not result in fully developed voices.

In this school of thought, the English tradition of instructing tenor voices is quite similar to instructing female voices. The cathedral tone is taught to lighter tenor voices. This tone, as previously described, is a pure tone without focus (the result of a great deal of breath being allowed to enter the tone) and lacking vibrato. The tone is focused in a manner similar to the German tradition, incorporating the idea of back, up, and over. Though this tone has been considered a "pure" tone, it is actually a tone that is quite controlled and manipulated. A singer who focuses the voice on just one area of resonance, while holding tension in the throat to suppress vibrato, is doing quite the opposite of pure singing and can cause detriment to vocal health (Bunch, 2005). In order to stop the voice from vibrating, the throat must be held to stop too much air from passing through the vocal folds. This does not allow the vocal mechanism to function naturally and, over time, will cause damage. Reid (1972) indicates:

> It cannot be stated too emphatically that the vibrato is of inestimable importance to good singing. Yet it must always be remembered that, like so many other phases of the vocal art, it cannot be regulated or controlled without injurious effect." (p. 176)

Vibrato is a natural occurrence in singing, "resulting from nerve impulse and coordinated muscular equilibrium" (Miller, 1986, p. 187). The cathedral or straight tone is not a pure tone in singing, since vibrato is "a natural ingredient of vocal timbre unless is it purposely eliminated in order to meet the criteria of certain cultural aesthetics or stylistic considerations" (p. 188). The English singer in the tradition of early baroque music was asked to remove vibrato from his sound to imitate the instrumentation that often accompanied this genre of music.

The English methodology for breath instruction is the same for male and female students. Breath is generally taken high in the ribs and back, with some singers lifting the shoulder blades. Due to the slightly more energized approach to breath support than that noted in the French tradition, larger tenor voices do exist in this national school. A more athletic approach to breath instruction results in operatic tenors with a full sound similar to the tone experienced in the Italian tradition. English composers of opera and oratorio repertoire such as Handel put great demands on singers. "It is impossible to conceive of nonvibrant singing of bravura tenor or bass arias, which were often written to be performed in competition with trumpets (a combination beloved by Handel)" (Miller, 1996, p. 130). The full lyric tenor tonal quality at times exhibits traces of tension and air in the sound, as the breath is generally taken in quite high in the sternum. This may interfere with the vocal mechanism functioning properly in a relaxed position. As well, the influence of the cathedral tone is found in this tradition, although it is less prevalent in the operatic genre.

The next section explores the national schools of singing as they apply to the baritone and bass voice. The tenets for the lowest of the male voices are quite similar to those instructed for other voice categories found in the German, French, English and Italian traditions for their female counterparts.

BARITONE AND BASS VOICES

The lyric baritone voice represents the most commonly found category of male singer in the German tradition. The tone of the lyric baritone, as with the tenor and with all voice types, is determined by physical characteristics such as the length of the neck, circumference of the chest, and dimensions of the

Adam's apple (for males). The male voice in particular does not reach its maturation until well after higher education studies. It is not uncommon to find a dramatic or spinto baritone mature to become a full lyric tenor, just as a large lyric or spinto mezzo-soprano may mature to become a dramatic soprano after higher education studies.

The German tradition of instructing this lower male voice is to encourage much darkening and dampening of the tone. This tone is accomplished as other German singers are instructed, with the image of something pushing down the back of the tongue to open the back of the throat. The range for the lowest bass in the German tradition is generally small. With so much pressure placed on the tongue to produce the desired heavy, dark sound, the vocal folds and larynx cannot move freely to facilitate a large vocal range. The concept of covering is also taught to the bass and baritone voices much as the female and tenor voices are instructed. This involves vowel modification as the range increases. It can be described as modifying an "ah" [a] vowel to an "oo" [u]. This maintains the image of something in the back of the throat with the tone focused primarily to the back of the throat, then up and over. The [u] vowel is what is known as a back vowel, as it is produced at the back of mouth with the palate lowered.

The result of covering the vocal tone is a smaller range with less brilliance and warmth in the tone that one might experience with an Italian baritone or bass, although Miller (1997) indicates the pure lyric baritone is able to negotiate similar repertoire to his Italian colleague. The traditional tone is very prevalent in most German male voices instructed in the national tradition, much as it is encountered with German voices of other categories. It is possible to sing the [u] vowel with brilliance and brightness in the tone, as one discovers when listening to a singer from the Italian tradition. The palate and mask remain lifted and one is able to see the roundness of the cheeks in a mirror. This keeps the sound focused forward, and incorporates more resonating chambers than when pulling the vowel back.

Technical tenets of instructing the baritone and bass voices in the Italian tradition parallel the national tradition of other Italian voice categories. The baritone and bass use the *appoggio* approach to breathing, with a balance of muscular activity and release, and strive towards maintaining a full, resonant tone throughout the vocal range. Miller notes that the large voice of the dramatic bass also embraces a great deal of brilliance and focus in his tone (1997). As in other vocal categories using an Italian approach to singing, the tone is generally well placed, the body is tension free, and the breath is cyclical and balanced.

The French tradition of instruction for males appears to produce a high number of light baritone voices. This may not be surprising, based on the background information presented on the pedagogical principles of vocal instruction historically in France. The natural approach to singing with little breath support combined with a preference for placing the vocal tone in the nasal passages results in lighter voices with a smaller range. Similarly, one does not find many large lyric or dramatic soprano or mezzo-soprano voices in this national school of thought. It is noted that the large number of lyric baritone voices is not due to physical characteristics of males divergent from those of the German, English, or Italian singer, but it is perhaps due to the lack of athleticism in approach to breath technique (Miller, 1997). One does not encounter as many dramatic or dark bass voices as one does in the German or Italian tradition.

The English approach to instructing the bass and baritone voice follows the same principles as other voice categories in this tradition. There are two branches of instruction: the cathedral tone previously discussed, and a technique that moves slightly toward an Italian technique for operatic repertoire. The English tenor is more renowned and specialised in the history of the national schools of singing. The English bass and baritone present close ties to the Italian School, in that there appears to be a more balanced and open tone than one finds with the lighter English tenor voices.

CONCLUSION

Some of the national schools of thought may place more focus on maintaining a national sound rather than thinking of vocal health and producing the most vibrant and full sound possible. The German tradition of singing, for example, strives to maintain a traditional German sound—dark, round and very controlled. Perhaps it was thought that this was required to sing the German repertoire appropriately. The idea of a great deal of control of the vocal tone and breath may contribute to inconsistency in singing. A student who is attempting to constrain his or her instrument may feel discomfort and experience hoarseness from placing pressure on the larynx. This method of singing may contribute to the prevalence of inconsistent singing and inhibit emotional performances.

The French tradition of singing places a great deal of emphasis on text and the interpretation of poetry in song texts. This focus is quite beneficial for a student to gain the ability to make individual and personal interpretations of text. The limitation of the French tradition of singing is the lack of focus placed on appropriate breath support, consistency though the full vocal range, and the prevalence of a light vocal tone without much resonance. This relaxed approach to vocal technique inhibits full development of the voice and will likely contribute to further inconsistency in singing for students.

The English tradition also appears to strive to maintain a national tradition of singing similar to the German School. The choral tradition and perhaps the notion of the cathedral tone furthers unemotional singing. The cathedral tone does not encourage an individual sound and places the focus on the music and not the individual interpretation of text. A voice that sounds like a cathedral tone is not an individual sound. The choral tradition is about blending and sounding as one voice. As well, withholding vibrato, and keeping the voice contained, as well as using high sternum breathing, will further inconsistent singing. The ways in which these traditional ideas are executed are through holding, restriction, and constriction. These will cause tension, fatigue, and further inconsistency in singing.

The Italian tradition of singing appears to be the method that will encourage consistency in singing. There is a general consensus in research that the Italian tradition of bel canto singing is the most balanced approach (Appelman, 1974; Caruso and Tetrazzini, 1975; Marchesi, 1970; Miller, 1977, 1986, 1997; Reid, 1972; Stark, 1999; Vennard, 1967). The notions of balance in breath, registration, brilliance in the vocal tone, and tension-free singing can help to contribute to consistency in singing when used as a teaching method in higher education. If facilitated well and with clear and concise instruction by a voice teacher, this method can be beneficial for a student. Perhaps if a student finds a consistent and comfortable way to sing, he or she can have the opportunity to emotionally connect to a piece of music.

It is essential to instruct using a teaching method that encourages consistency in singing for students, thus leading to their ability to emotionally engage in a piece of music instead of being distracted by vocal problems or discomfort. In the next section, several pedagogical approaches to vocal instruction will be examined. Some of the following methods may attempt to use an Italian approach to vocal instruction, striving for tension-free singing; however, what will be noted is that the manner in which this information is translated to a student is quite important. A vocal instructor may have the best intentions of instructing using a method based in the Italian tradition, but if the information is not facilitated in a way that a student can understand and rely on, the problem of inconsistency and lack of engagement will continue.

PEDAGOGICAL APPROACHES IN HIGHER EDUCATION INSTITUTIONS

There are conflicting approaches as well as inherent difficulties in describing vocal instruction. As will be discussed in this section, various approaches to teaching voice exist. Approaches for vocal instruction may be those based in science and anatomy, those based in imagery and visualization, a natural approach, a holistic approach, or other approaches considered contemporary, in that they have been created in the past fifty years. Some teachers may attempt to instruct with an overlap of several styles or adhere to just one method.

It is a challenge to describe a standardised approach to vocal instruction. Fields (1947) outlined several difficulties that illustrate how a standardized approach is relatively impossible to describe. He described difficulties such as the subjective nature of singing. Singing involves self-analysis as well as analysis by the instructor, and both singer and instructor may have a different opinion of what he or she hears. Another difficulty noted is that many authorities on voice and vocal instruction disagree. This will be evident in the sections describing various national approaches as well as overarching teaching tenets in higher education music institutions. Additionally, there is a lack of standards for, and regulation of, voice teaching. One does not find a standardized board exam or other ways of certifying the depth and breadth of knowledge of voice teachers, as is found in other professions. Many voice teachers use an individual method without testing it empirically for success or failure, and simply continue to teach using the same approach. Some voice instructors at the higher education level may engage in active performing careers or have a substantial list of performance credits on their curricula vitae; however, these individuals may not be able to facilitate the acquisition of technique and artistry for their students.

This confusion, conflict, and variation in approaches present a challenge to the student trying to navigate the process of finding his or her vocal sound and building a technique that will result in artistic performances.

The various pedagogical approaches to instructing voice in North American institutions are not considered part of a national school of thought. This is due to the concept that many teachers based in North American institutions come from various backgrounds and teaching traditions that have been blended with new traditions in North America (Blades-Zeller, 2003). This is in direct contrast to the western European national schools of thought, in which teachers adhere to national pedagogical tenets when instructing voice students. Much of the pedagogical tradition in North American institutions stems from the Italian tradition (Blades-Zeller, 2003; Clements, 2008; Deere, 2002; Dufault, 2008; Miller 1977, 1997; Stark, 1999; Sell, 2005; Taylor 1922). Influences from several national schools are found in North America. The English and German choral traditions are represented in Canada and the United States. As well "there exists an open rivalry in some regions of Canada between the Italian and the German techniques" (Miller, 1997, p. 202).

A group of voice instructors from higher education institutions in the United States were surveyed as to whether or not they felt there is an American vocal sound or school of thought (Blades-Zeller, 2003). Teachers surveyed indicated that no American national school of singing exists, describing an American sound or voice stamp as "natural," "fresh," "versatile," "non-mannered," or "Italianate style" (pp.185 and 187). Only one teacher surveyed felt there is an American sound, which she described as forward and bright. One of the female instructors (in Blades-Zeller, 2003) states, "The best American-trained singer uses the traditional Italian or bel canto method" (p. 190). Several teachers described the German sound quite negatively: a female instructor indicates, "Germans do a lot of barking" (p.

186), while another female instructor described the German sound as "narrow" (p. 188). Several instructors surveyed described their method of instruction in institutions as being influenced by Italian or German techniques.

There are numerous pedagogical approaches to teaching voice. For instance, terms such as a "mechanistic approach" were more prominent in the early 20th century; however, this approach lacks the physiological aspect and use of technology found in today's scientific approach to teaching (Deere, 2002; Fields, 1947).

Notions of vocal instruction can be classified as: mechanistic (technical, scientific), poetic (imagery based teaching), psychological (historically referred to as visual or based in imagery), demonstrative (rote teaching), empirical (experimental teaching while rejecting vocal science), phonetic (training the singer as one would speak), progressive (using vocal literature as a teaching tool), inspirational (imprinting behavior from teacher to student; parallels demonstrative), holistic (attempting to unify all aspects of the singer), natural (the "do-nothing" approach), technical (similar to mechanistic), technically intense (mechanistic), interpretation-oriented (avoiding technical aspects and studying literature; similar to progressive and natural approaches), the technique-mystique teacher (imagery; parallels poetic), the one-aspect teacher (teacher focused on one part of singing exclusive of other aspects), meditation (meditation as a means to remove tensions), and removing muscular interferences (tension-free singing; parallels natural, meditation, and phonetic approaches) (Bruser, 2011; Clements, 2008; Dufault, 2008; Deere, 2002; Elliot, 2010; Fields, 1947; Gregg, 2001; Miller, 1986; Nelson & Blades, 2005; Samoiloff, 1942; Stark, 1999). Additionally, in current vocal instruction, pedagogical methods such as Speech Level Singing™ (2020), Estill Voice Training™ (2020), Somatic Voicework™, The LoVetri Method (2020), the International Voice Teachers of Mix (2020), and the mindfulness of the Feldenkrais Method® (2020) exist. For the purpose of review for this research study, several commonly used approaches for vocal instruction in higher education institutions will be selected, as well as the contemporary methods listed above. The approaches that will be reviewed are those based in vocal science and anatomy, imagery and imagination, a natural approach, a holistic approach, and several very contemporary teaching approaches. Some similar and distinguishing characteristics will be presented, as well as their relation to tenets that parallel the national schools described in the previous section of this study.

Vocal Science and Anatomy

The first pedagogical approach that will be examined is a method based in the use of vocal science and anatomy as the foundation for instruction. This method involves the use of explanations of how the vocal mechanism functions and knowledge of the anatomy of the vocal mechanism. The first teacher credited with using a scientific approach to vocal instruction is Manuel Garcia (1835). Garcia was the teacher first credited with a more scientific approach to vocal pedagogy and with the development of the *laryngoscope* (an instrument which allows one to see the vocal folds and glottis), which is significant for maintaining vocal health (Clements, 2008; Deere, 2002; Reid, 1972; Stark, 1999; Ware, 1998). David (1995) writes of the change of focus in vocal instruction, indicating that, historically, "voice teachers have remained happily uniformed about the workings of the larynx and vocal tract" (p. xi). Garcia took a more scientific look at the vocal mechanism and its function: "When Garcia invented his laryngoscope, new curiosities were aroused as to the probable nature of the vocal function and its mechanics" (Reid, 1972, p. 3). Many teachers reacted against this more scientific approach (Clements, 2008).

There are teaching methodologies influenced by the science and physiology of singing currently used in some higher education institutions in North America. "A new voice pedagogy is emerging which is based on an understanding of the structure and function of the vocal and respiratory tracts" (David, 1995, p. xii). The conceptual underpinning of a methodology based in vocal science is the premise that a voice teacher who has knowledge of how the voice functions will teach in a way that promotes vocal health and longevity in singing. Some teachers use technological tools such as a voice spectrograph or other software-based programs to aid in a visual representation of the voice. These tools will be discussed in further detail. A scientific teaching approach based on the physiology and anatomy of the vocal mechanism is a preventative method. Its central tenets surround vocal health and avoidance of abuse, as well as the identification of vocal problems. David notes that "knowledge has evolved into a systematic understanding of proper voice use in order to avoid laryngeal damage before it happens" (p. xii). Voice professors who instruct at higher education institutions have increased scientific awareness of the physiological aspects of singing and how tone is produced (Alderson, 1979; Appelman, 1974; Bunch, 1997, Doscher, 1994; McKinney, 1994; Ware, 1998).

Certain prominent higher education music institutes [10] and well-known vocal pedagogues promote the usage of vocal science as part of their teaching curriculum (Miller, 1977, 1986, 1997, 2004; Blades-Zeller, 2003; Bunch, 1997; Doscher, 1994; McKinney, 1994; McPherson, 2002; Sataloff, 1998).

The implementation of technology such as a voice spectrograph in the voice studio is considered a potentially important addition to vocal instruction

---

[10] Vocal Arts Center of Oberlin University, Westminster Choir College Voice Research Center, Syracuse University, University of Florida, University of Iowa, Northwestern University, University of Arizona and the Denver Center for Performing Arts.

(Barnes-Burrow et al., 2008; Callaghan & Wilson, 2004; Miller, 2008; Titze, 1986). Titze (1994) indicates, "If we believe the statement that singing is vocal athletics, we could perhaps benefit from experiences that the field of athletics has had with high technology" (p. 276). Titze sees technology as a way to chart changes in student progress and as a way to address vocal health issues as soon they occur. As well, he sees technology in the voice studio as a way to increase efficiency in singing as well as to move towards a standardized approach to instructing singing.

Some voice instructors indicate their use of technology as a teaching aid. It is used to offer instant feedback and assessment to the teacher and student. Glaros (2006), for example, details numerous technological tools she uses as teaching aids. She lists recording devices such as digital recorders and CD burners to record lessons, the use of Webcams for visual feedback, and a computer to show students videos of songs they are studying. As well, she discusses music software that scans music to a computer and plays digital vocal accompaniment tracks, such as SmartMusic® and Finale®. The SmartMusic® program plays vocal accompaniment tracks and has the ability to alter tempo (speed). It also has a recording function, whereby the student can record her practice session of a particular song for playback. There are other software programs that offer auto-accompanying and some vocal anthologies come with karaoke accompaniment CDs. These may be of benefit while learning a new song or they may help the student internalise the piano accompaniment for a song; however, it does seem more beneficial for the teacher and/or accompanist to work in person with the student to find the most individualised interpretation of a song. Each student must find a fitting tempo, and the unique interpretation of a song text and melodic line cannot be practiced independently by a student using an accompaniment CD. The student will inevitably follow along with the CD and will not set her own tempo. If the student continues to use a karaoke CD, this interpretation as well as tempo is what will be set in the muscle memory of the student in the practice room. As well, the collaborative relationship of the singer and pianist is an artistic interaction that simply cannot be replicated by a technological tool.

Glaros (2006) believes this software program is quite valuable in its ability to record the student singing pre-set vocal exercises. The student sings vocal exercises that are part of the software program. They are recorded and the assessment given to the student entails noting accuracy or errors in pitch and rhythm. These files can be saved and emailed to the vocal instructor.

Though it is quite important for a student to learn the pitches and rhythms of a song or vocal exercise accurately, this software program will not help facilitate consistent vocal technique, and thus may not improve the ability to sing artistically. This use of technology may help the singer consistently sing in tune and be aware of rhythm; however, it will not aid the student in mitigating the challenge of finding a consistent resonant singing tone. An instructional method utilizing a software program such as this one, with assessment tools for pitch and rhythm as well as pre-determined vocal exercises, does not address the singer as an individual. Each student may not benefit from the same exercises, as each student may have different issues to address. No one singer is the same as another or has the same areas of vocal development to work on. Pre-determined exercises may not address specific needs and may not foster consistent singing. The student who is instructed with a method incorporating such software will be encouraged to focus on accurate rhythm and pitch. This may not facilitate consistency in singing and will not likely foster artistry. If a student is instructed to primarily focus on rhythm and pitch, it is apparent that there is not much focus on expressiveness and an emotional connection to the music and text. As well, vocal instructors should tailor individual exercises for their students based on what issues must be addressed. Instant assessment and a flexible approach must be used. This cannot be accomplished if a student emails a set of vocal exercises to the voice instructor.

Some voice instructors at higher education institutions state that knowledge of vocal science is part of an outstanding teacher skill set. One of male instructors surveyed (2009) writes, "It is imperative to recognise that knowledge of the voice mechanism and its foundation of objective pedagogy. A mastery of these concepts is prerequisite for artistic expression" (p. 106). Another instructor interviewed (in Blades-Zeller, 2003) states, "By far at the head of the list, is to know your field. Know how the voice functions" (p. 221). One of the male instructors indicates, "Number one is the ability to diagnose a voice and diagnose vocal faults" (p. 222). An additional male instructor states, "An outstanding teacher has knowledge of the voice, the mechanism and how it works" (p. 223). As well, one of the female instructors states an attribute as "knowledge of the instrument, technical and in regard to repertoire," and another indicates that "we must have a knowledge of voice structure and function and how it all works together" (p. 224). Additionally, one of the male instructors reviewed states, "In our day and age, it's important for a teacher to have a solid knowledge of the anatomy and physiology of the voice" (p. 227). These instructors at higher education institutions consider knowledge of the anatomy of the voice and how it functions as an important part of higher education vocal instruction. It is of great value to a voice instructor to have knowledge of how the vocal mechanism functions. It gives the instructor the opportunity to explain the function of singing in a logical manner to the student. This can be aided with the use of anatomy diagrams. Singing is a blind activity. Singers do not have the opportunity to see how a note is emitted, as is possible for a pianist or cellist, for example. A voice teacher with the ability and capacity to illustrate how a note is phonated by the vocal mechanism, how the breath functions, as well as where the voice resonates in the body may help to foster consistent singing. This teacher will have the ability to give credible and relevant information to a student that a student can think about while practising between lessons. This information must, however, be executed while working with the student on artistic interpretation as well; otherwise, the instruction will be compartmentalised and will not address the entire singer.

Another method claimed to be a scientific approach is called the Vocal Science™ Method (2020). Proponents of this method claim it is able to promote accelerated vocal development. The Royans School of Vocal Science (2020), guarantees that students will be the ability to sing at a professional level in ten hours or less. Yampolsky indicates the method is a holistic method, because the body is viewed as the instrument and the singing voice is a reflection of the inner self. The mechanics of the teaching method incorporate repetitive exercises and visualization to help achieve proper vocal placement and to help pitch. It incorporates elements of posture and the use of facial and abdominal muscles. As well, the method employs the use of a PA system, keyboard, video camera, and microphone.

This particular method appears quite ambiguous and confusing. The method is called "vocal science," which would indicate instruction based in vocal anatomy and the mechanics of singing as one finds in a higher education vocal pedagogy course. The method also claims to be holistic and indicates that the body is the instrument. The resonating chambers of the face, skull, and vocal tract are where natural vocal resonance takes place. If this method is holistic—whereby the body is the instrument— it is not clear why the method uses a microphone and PA system. Artificial amplification of the voice (in a classical setting) is not a holistic approach, and it is not using the body as an instrument capable of natural acoustics and amplification. The method also uses posture as part of the teaching practice. As will be discussed in the review of a natural approach to vocal instruction, posture and alignment are part of a natural method. This method also incorporates the use of visualization, which is part of a methodology based in imagery and imagination but not vocal science. A voice teacher should have the ability to draw from a varied skill set; however, this method appears ambiguous. The use of repetitive exercises, as well as the use of artificial amplification, may not help a student find her individual resonant singing tone or consistency in singing. Moreover, the method does not appear to indicate how it may foster artistic and emotionally engaged singing.

Vocal science combined with the use of technology has been considered in some institutions as a way to assist students in certain technical aspects, such as finding a resonant singing tone and breath support. Rebecca Folsom (2011) suggests that it is necessary to divide what she considers the five parts of the physiology of singing— "the neurological utility, breathing, laryngeal function, resonance/vocal tract and articulation"—into separate components, instructing students about each facet individually to ensure students understand each component of the vocal mechanism (p. 404). While this knowledge may be beneficial, this approach may be too compartmentalised and might leave a student with no concept of a complete singer: person, body, mind, and soul.

Other instructors feel that a beneficial way to prepare new voice teachers is to ensure that they have studied a great deal of anatomy. Amanda Brunk (2008), for example, feels voice pedagogy students and those wishing to instruct voice should study vocal science. According to Brunk:

> The ideal situation would be that this new teacher has studied anatomy, physiology, and voice disorders pertinent to the function of the vocal mechanism and the body as an instrument. (p. 617)

Brunk's opinion as to how to prepare teachers in vocal pedagogy degree programs is that they should work in voice laboratories with acoustic analysis machines. She indicates several Canadian higher education institutions that offer one course in vocal pedagogy (study of vocal anatomy, and the physiology of the singing voice and how it functions). She expresses concern over the lack of vocal science study in many Canadian institutions, where students are "at a significant disadvantage for understanding the importance of voice science in today's teaching" (p. 616). She summarises her thoughts on the responsibility of a teacher to be one who has knowledge of the anatomy of the voice and can identify vocal health problems. She appears critical both of teachers with excellent artistic ability and a great many performing credits in their career and of teachers who do not have a strong foundation in vocal science and anatomy. Brunk's opinion suggests that she values scientific knowledge as more of an asset to instruction than the ability to demonstrate and facilitate artistic interpretation. Knowledge of vocal anatomy is quite beneficial for teachers; however, the relationship between the student and teacher is an important element and it is beneficial to prepare students to translate knowledge of vocal science as well as to facilitate artistic singing. There must be a balance in place.

Some higher education music schools have used technical tools as part of their pedagogy with the particular use of video voice lessons. Eberle (2003) feels that this form of technology will give distance students an opportunity to be part of a larger music community, as "video conferencing and web-based instruction will enrich our students' performance and creative work" (p. 244). She states further that "these supplemental educational tools can indeed enhance the teaching of voice" (p. 245). Though web-based instruction has value in many educational settings, the relationship in the voice studio between teacher and student, with teacher as facilitator, is a relationship based in personal interaction and trust that may lose some effectiveness with a technological barrier. As well, some instructors use a "hands on" approach while teaching breath support, for example. It may be necessary for a teacher to place his or her hands on the rib cage of the student to guide the student as to where to breathe. This cannot be accomplished via web-based lessons.

Technical tools that provide a visual aid to measure accuracy in pitch, resonance, and rate of vibrato have been considered a useful teaching aid. Callaghan and Wilson (2004) indicate, "Many studies have shown that feedback is an essential part of learning psychomotor skills and, since more than sixty percent of the population are visual learners, visual feedback is particularly effective "(p. 1). Callaghan and Wilson (2004) developed a software program to assist voice teachers in the instruction of technical elements such as pitch, breath management, proper phonation (production of clear vocal tone without breath in the sound), and resonance. The program is designed to provide sequential exercises with feedback from a computer as a visual aid. The teacher is to follow the program as indicated in the manual. A typical scientific approach to voice pedagogy may consist of pre-planned lessons and predetermined goals. Wurgler (1997) writes:

> Pre-service teachers write innumerable lesson plans in their education course to practice writing goals, finding appropriate materials, and translating goals and materials into sequential steps. Often the written plan includes preplanned key questions, readiness activities, optional teaching strategies and even scripted steps (what a teacher plans to say at each step). (p. 3)

This sequential framework provides little support for a teacher in finding the student's individual sound. The emphasis in this style of teaching is a form of repetitive teaching, without much flexibility. A teacher who has a set lesson plan or follows a manual with scripted steps for voice students limits the opportunities for the student to think for herself, since "the teacher must help the student make connections" (p. 5). If a teacher is not equipped with a way to help the student find her individual sound or consistent technique and merely has her repeating multiple vocal exercises without relevance, the student will be confused and likely discouraged. This methodology may have a result similar to the computer-based software programs that present sequential exercises showing errors in pitch and rhythm, but offer little to foster technical consistency or expressive singing.

Additional researchers such as Scherer et al. (1994) indicate the positive effect they believe technology may have as a teaching tool for voice:

> Imagine the increased power of our teaching tools if we could identify and utilize the physiological nuances of vocal function responsible for communicating most effectively such emotions as

scorn or sadness, mirth or happiness, in our professional and sometimes not so professional voice students. (p. 361)

This group of voice teachers, speech pathologists, and scientists discussed the effects of implementing more science and technology in working with the voice. Discussion group member Rubin states, "I can more readily identify vocal misuse, abuse, and disorders" (Scherer et al., 1994, p.365). Howell indicates, "We teachers need the help of the laryngologists and the speech pathologists and the scientists who continue to define our terminology" (p. 371). Much of the study revolves around vocal health and maintenance, better teaching terminology, more accurate measurement of registers, vibrato, and resonance. There is, however, no indication of the positive effect on artistic singing. If one spends numerous hours in voice lessons and the practice room solely viewing a laptop or monitor when does the singer have the opportunity to explore artistry in text and character?

Other studies have been conducted by researchers measuring how much use of technology is present in the voice studio. Barnes-Burroughs, Lan, Edwards, Noe, and Archambeault (2008) surveyed voice instructors in the United States regarding their use of and attitudes towards technology in the teaching studio. Teachers were questioned on their usage of several forms of technology, such as pitch-matching software, vocal methods and technique software, sound recording software, and music teaching computer software. Of the 52 teachers who responded to the survey, twenty-four were instructors in higher education institutions. A range of 80% to 98% of the total number of teachers surveyed indicated having no experience with the use of technology in the voice studio. It is interesting to note that this does indicate that there are some higher education teachers using some form of computer software as a teaching aid in their studios.

Tools such as voice spectrographs can be used in a pedagogical approach based in science and anatomy. The use of spectrographs offers a means of instant assessment to a teacher and singer during a lesson. The concept of resonance, considered in a scientific approach to pedagogy, can be instructed using a microphone placed at the lips of the singer. Acoustic resonance can be measured with a visual representation instantly available on screen to assess the frequency of the sound. This method is considered a teaching tool as well as a method of assessment for both the student and the instructor. It adds a level of real-time feedback and data collection, and it measures resonance. A student can relate the feeling of resonating to a visual tool to validate this sensation during a lesson. Epps, Smith and Wolfe (1997) performed a study measuring acoustic resonance in the vocal tract for the speaking voice using a non-invasive method of measurement for male and female voices. The vocal folds send an excitement signal through the vocal tract, which is measured by placing a microphone in front of the singer's mouth to pick up the frequency emitted.

A study by Joliveau, Smith, and Wolfe (2004) continued this method of measuring resonance in singers by engaging in a study measuring the acoustic resonance of a soprano. In this experiment, a microphone was placed at the mouth of the singer. Diagram 1 shows how acoustic resonance was measured in a non-invasive manner. An example of an invasive test of acoustic resonance is to have a singer lean into a megaphone type apparatus and attempt to sing in a natural manner. Leaning to sing into a megaphone type of apparatus will cause the singer to have her neck out of alignment, thus changing the shape of the vocal tract and affecting resonance. The following example illustrates a way to measure resonance in which the singer can maintain posture conducive to good singing.

Diagram 1

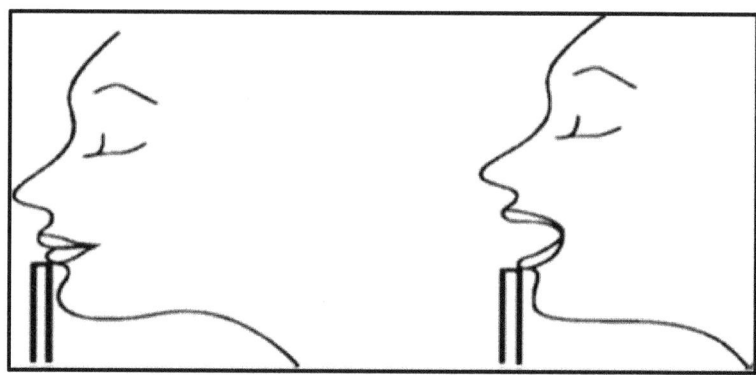

(Joliveau et al. 2004, p. 2435)

The measurement of frequency and the visual image of a graph represent the amount of resonance emitted by the singer. The use of such technological tools can be beneficial in building consistency in singing when used in a lesson with both teacher and student present. The student has the opportunity to connect a sensation of resonance with visual feedback indicating if the tone is emitting a frequency that falls within the range of "ring." This range occurs between 2000-3000Hz. A singer whose voice resonates in this range has the ability to be heard above an orchestra without amplification (Sundberg, 1977).

Some teachers in higher education institutions agree that a certain amount of knowledge of vocal science and anatomy is beneficial. Higher education voice instructor Helding (2012), indicates, "As an organization of voice professionals, we should likewise be grateful that there are those among us who are called to understand the construction of the vocal fold at the cellular level" (p. 67). Simonson (2012) reviews newer research topics in the field of voice for the past few years. Much research in higher education music departments is surrounding the use of science and technology in the voice studio. Topics have included measuring vocal registers using software programs, acoustical analysis of the tenor voice, and analysis of the voice for speaking versus singing. In the *Journal of Singing,* a new category has been present in past years entitled "Voice Research and Technology" (Titze, 2011). This represents the idea that knowledge of science and anatomy, as well the use of technology, is becoming more mainstream in vocal instruction.

Other researchers, such as Kirkpatrick, a higher education voice instructor, and McLester, an exercise physiologist (2012), studied and implemented the use of EMG (electromyographic) feedback to instruct singers to sing with a low laryngeal position. Perhaps it best that the singer become kinaesthetically aware of how it feels to sing with a lowered larynx rather than needing or relying on the feedback of a computer?

In an article reviewing the past twenty-five years of vocal instruction, Cleveland (1994) tracked changes in certain technical aspects of singing, including views on resonance, registers, vibrato, and voice classification. He also reviewed what he considered the most important technological developments, such as spectrograph analysis for real-time viewing of vocal function. He summarised by stating the most significant change in twenty-five years: "We have seen a divided community of teachers, researchers, medical doctors, and speech-language pathologists, people who once worked in total isolation, realize their common interests can be better served by uniting and teaching and learning from each other" (p. 23). He writes of the collaboration between voice professionals and scientists as the possibility of "a gigantic technological transfer of information and knowledge from laboratory to the teaching studio, and a transfer of instrumental technology to assist in the studio" (p. 23). Perhaps a positive outcome to be considered from a pedagogy based in science is an increased awareness by the student and pedagogue of vocal health and the prevention of vocal damage. Visual feedback on certain technical aspects of singing is also beneficial; however, this does not advance artistic singing or interpretation and emphasises just one aspect of singing.

Some concern has been expressed by voice teachers that the focus of voice pedagogy has been based solely on the physiology of singing. Denes Striny (2007, 2011) discusses his worry about the nature of voice pedagogy and its focus on the science and physiology of singing with little emphasis on ease of tone production. He expresses his fear that students will have a hard time finding a competent teacher. Miller (1986) states, "American vocal pedagogy has become a body with two heads, one speaking with the voice of the subjective teacher, the other with the voice of the science-oriented teacher" (p. 209).

It is apparent that a pedagogy based solely in science may consider just one aspect of voice student instruction without addressing other important aspects, such as artistic interpretation of music or the opportunity for voice teachers in higher education institutions to give students individualised attention. It is beneficial for the voice instructor to be able to translate clear and concise explanations of how the voice functions to his or her students. This may aid in fostering consistent singing for the student during practice sessions between voice lessons. If the student knows how the voice functions, he or she can approach studying the technique of singing well versed in how the vocal mechanism works. This must be combined, however, with an artistic interpretation of text.

The use of technological tools can be helpful as a means of instant feedback when used in the voice studio during a lesson. The instructor can help the student make the connections of a physical awareness of sound to visual feedback. This may, however, only be successful during a lesson, unless the student also possesses an apparatus to use for his or her individualised practice sessions. Muscle memory requires repetition. Using a tool such as a spectrograph in a weekly lesson will not give the student enough time to retain the awareness of the singing tone and to remember how to replicate it in a practice room. The majority of student work, practice, and implementation of the muscle memory of vocal technique will take place alone in the practice room. The use of technology as a means of instruction can only be successful if the teacher is constantly present with a spectrograph or other tool for feedback. Relying on a technological tool during a lesson will not help a student gain long term consistency in singing and will not foster independent awareness for the student while practicing. As well, a technological tool will have no benefit for a student attempting to make an emotional connection to the music.

It is also important to consider that if the student is instructed merely as the sum of her physiological components of singing, there can be little individualised attention. An instructor who uses scripted or sequential exercises gauging feedback through technology may not be addressing the individual needs of the student. As well, if the primary focus of instruction is on just the anatomy and mechanics of singing and does not address the individual and the artistic, emotional, and interpretive aspects of singing, the approach can be considered standardized. I believe instructing the higher education singer holistically is a more beneficial approach, in which there is a component of scientific knowledge of how the vocal mechanism functions and can help the student make the connection of correct usage of the vocal mechanism that can be practiced between lessons. This must be balanced by the instructor fostering individual creative expression and interpretation of music and text.

The next section will explore the use of imagery and imagination as a method of vocal instruction in higher education voice studios. This approach is in direct contrast to a scientific approach, as little to no explanation of how the voice functions is used during instruction. The lack of explanation of how the voice functions may cause students to use their instruments incorrectly and may also cause confusion for the student attempting to build consistency in singing in a practice room alone.

Imagery and Imagination

A second category of voice pedagogy considered in higher education institutions is a methodology based in imagery and imagination. It is unrelated to a scientific approach, as instruction is based on visual images presented to students as opposed to physiological and mechanical explanations of how the breath mechanism functions, how to produce vocal tone, and how to resonate the vocal tone. Imagery and imagination have been used as methods of instruction (Blades-Zeller, 2003; Clements, 2008; McKinney, 1994; Miller, 1986, 1997; Samoiloff, 1942; Smithrim, 2003; Stark, 1999; Vennard, 1967). There is considerable debate on the use of imagery in the field of higher education instruction. "Imagery and the use of images to develop vocal technique is an area in which there is as much controversy as there is interest" (Blades-Zeller, 2003). Imagery is an approach whereby a teacher presents an image for a student to consider, hoping that the end result will be the desired singing tone. Bunch (2005) discusses the difficulty in finding a resonant singing tone, "the quality of the human voice that is unique with every individual; and at the same time, it is the most difficult to study and quantify" (p. 68). Bunch suggests students have a "vivid imagination" in order to learn to find a resonant singing tone (p. 70).

Historically, a teaching approach based in imagery was a rebellion against the scientific approach presented by Garcia and other pedagogues using science-based teaching practices (Clements, 2008; Miller, 1997; Reid, 1972; Stark, 1999). Reid (1972) states, "The advance of technology and the advent of the scientific era, the proponents of Bel Canto training were left defenceless" (p. 4). Teachers who were resistant to change argued against science, and "a new generation of teachers came along to confront a world in a process of change" (p. 4).

Imagery is at times used in vocal instruction to convey breath technique to students. Blades-Zellers' (2003) observations of higher education voice instructors indicated some images used by the instructors for breath instruction. Examples of images included "describe the breath much like a swimmer's breath" (p. 94), or an image of a steel tube through which the student must visualise his or her breath. Other instructors presented images such as "breathe as if you are pleasantly surprised about something" (p. 98).

Further images for how to breathe were explained as "image the body as a balloon to be expanded," or "breathing in through one-hundred noses located on a belt around the waist," and "breathing into the arms, legs, neck or other parts of the body" (p.24).

These images may not give a student a clear and pragmatic indication of how to inhale and expand the rib cage by allowing the diaphragm muscle to lower at the base of the rib cage. Perhaps if a student were shown an illustration of the diaphragm muscle in a relaxed position shaped as a cap, combined with an explanation of the mechanics of the diaphragm muscle lowering and expanding, it might give a clearer indication of a low abdominal breath and how the ribs expand.

Some instructors in institutions use a pedagogical approach based in imagery to instruct resonance in the singing tone. Edwin (2011) describes how he uses the image of a pear to teach resonance to voice students. He states, "In voice pedagogy circles, the term 'pear-shaped tone' has fallen into disuse. Popular in the nineteenth and twentieth centuries, the phrase describes a tone that is full, clear, warm, and resonant" (p. 193). Edwin continues, "No matter whether the vocal pear is small, medium, or large, it is important for every singer to explore all of his or her pear" (p. 194). This use of imagery and, in particular, the visual image of a round tone draws some parallels to the tenets described in the German national school of singing whereby students are instructed to think of their tone as round and are presented with the image of a rounded piece of fruit in their throats to accomplish this tone.

Katharine Smithrim (2003), writing of how she was instructed by a female voice teacher, she makes the assumption that "all singing teachers use imagery to communicate ideas about the physical process of singing" (p. 56). Yet clearly all teachers do not use imagery and some may choose a more holistic approach. She describes the "hidden pedagogy" (p. 56) of her lessons. She writes how her instructor tells her to "wash her face with sound" (p. 56), she was to rub her face, and to hum while pretending to wash her face. The instructor presents this image as a way to teach Smithrim resonance, but without Smithrim being aware that she was learning how to resonate her voice. She gives an image of how to sing high notes. She indicates that Smithrim should "imagine that the sound was coming out of the top of my head and to use my hand flying off my head to help me visualize the physical process" (p. 56). This was supposed to teach Smithrim to relax her jaw so she could sing high notes. Using this imagery raises the question of why a teacher would not simply ask the student to relax her jaw and let her experience that feeling of relaxation. Smithrim describes several approaches to singing a correct ah [a] vowel. Her instructor tells her to sing an ah [a] vowel, "as if you were looking at two little kittens curled up on a pillow" (p. 56) or as if "you just discovered you had locked your keys in the car, now as if you were walking alone at night and something brushed against your arm" (p. 56). This "hidden pedagogy" is intended to teach one to relax the tongue, lips, and throat; however, without a clear indication of the goal from an instructor, it may not result in relaxation.

Eloise Ristad (1982) gives workshops for musicians. She uses imagery in her workshops, presenting such ideas as asking students to stretch out on the floor to try to find a resonant singing tone. One soprano was encouraged to balance on her head to find her resonant, ringing tone, then instructed to imagine the same feeling when standing. Other images and ideas given to singers were to try to "sing it ugly," try to "sound shrill," "drink the sound," "sing on the interest not the capital," "think horizontally," and then in other cases, "think vertically." These ideas are intended to aid in singing tension free and technically correct (1982). It is unclear how instructing a student to try to sound bad or shrill will promote consistent singing. These images are contradicting the type of sound a student should attempt to make. They are confusing and ambiguous.

Several of the higher education voice instructors Blades-Zeller (2003) surveyed were asked about the use of imagery to instruct singing with a resonant singing tone. Some instructors indicated they used images such as, "smile under or behind the eyes" (p. 87) or suggested that a student should think "up and over" (p. 94). Other instructors attempted to instruct resonance through imagery by suggesting that a student should "let that sound go out over her glasses" (p. 89) or imagine that "sometimes the sound is like a waterfall going backward in your throat" (p. 96). Students were told to "imagine you are singing out the back of your head" (p. 99). Other ambiguous ideas presented to students about resonance were to think of the vocal tone as the point of a triangle or as curves or squares, or to imagine the vocal tone as a piece of wire that must carry current. These images are supposed to instruct the student in how to place or focus the tone. An additional image presented suggested that a student should think "he/she is eating a hot pizza and doesn't want the cheese to stick to the roof of the mouth" (p. 95). This image is supposed to help a student lift the palate, although it is unclear how a student can make a connection between the image of hot pizza and lifting the palate. Some of these images—for example the idea of singing out of the back of the head— show parallels to ideas presented in the German national school of thought. As discussed earlier, some of the tenets of the German school promote control, pressure at the back of the throat, and constriction of the sternum. These may cause tension in the throat and will likely not help consistency in singing. With many of the images presented to students, their creators do not consider how a student may be able to use the same image to replicate the same sound in a practice room.

An image may help a student sing a correct tone during a lesson with the guidance of a teacher; however, without making a concrete connection to the image and understanding how to physically reproduce the same tone in a practice room, a student may not be able to sing in the same manner. If mistakes occur, the student will be imprinting incorrect muscle memory. Wei (2006) reviewed a study testing the effect imagery-based teaching by several higher education instructors has on pitch accuracy, sound pressure level, and singing power ratio. This was tested with the use of acoustic analysis. The results showed that although some students responded to imagery during lessons, the use of imagery as a methodology had no prevailing effect on pitch, sound pressure, and power in singing.

The use of imagery may cause confusion for an inexperienced student and may not be a beneficial pedagogical approach to use in the voice studio. Deirdre Michael writes (2011):

> The use of imagery is a time-honored method of teaching singing, but many useful images are actually at odds with physiologic reality. The problem is that some singers will confuse imagery with reality and base their technique on a concept that was useful as an image, but dangerous as a core belief. This seems especially true with concepts that are formed early in the development of singing, and then followed subconsciously throughout the development of the mature technique. It may behoove us, as singing teachers, to differentiate between images and physiologic reality, so that our students use their images more appropriately. (p. 417)

The unique singing tone of each person must be based on an individual physical awareness and a sensation and experience of where the voice is vibrating. The student must have something concrete to rely on in order to be able to practice this behavior.

Many higher education voice instructors do not believe that vocal instruction based in imagery is particularly successful. The following are several examples. My former teacher, Patricia Misslin (1997), did not use a great deal of imagery in instruction. If she spoke of imagery, it was only in relation to interpretation of text and music. The central tenets of her teaching methodology were based in an individualised interpretation of text and the acquisition of strong musicianship. Her technical approach was quite natural, as I will review in the next section of pedagogical approaches. One of the male instructors (in Blades-Zellar, 2003) states, "I use very little imagery because I find that unless the students can hook into what you mean by that image, it doesn't mean much" (p.88). Another indicates, "For technical matters, I speak in general to the muscles, not the brain" (p. 92). One of the male instructors interviewed says" the voice is an acoustic and physical instrument, it is not correct, in my viewpoint, to make up imagery about physical and acoustic process because those factors are factual" (p. 87). A female instructor indicates, "All learning is sensory based? We learn by what we feel, hear and see" (p. 92). These instructors believe that instructing a student how to use the muscles related to a resonant singing tone with clear explanations is a better approach than the use of imagery. The use of imagery for the purpose of text interpretation can be beneficial. Often song texts are poems or a depiction of the emotions of a character. Imagery and imagination can be beneficial for a student trying to make an emotional connection to a poem by visualising the scene or character.

One does not find similar characteristics in an approach based in vocal science and anatomy and one based in imagery. They are quite distinct. An instructor who uses a scientific approach instructs technique based on the mechanics of the voice and how it functions, perhaps incorporating the use of a voice spectrograph or other technology. An instructor using an approach based in imagery presents students with images that must be translated by the student to vocal technique. A disconnect is apparent in using a pedagogical approach based solely in imagery. The student may have difficulty connecting a visual or verbal image to an actual kinesthetic sensation of tone or to the idea of how to use his or her breath. A more literal or physiological explanation of how the voice functions may result in clearer physical awareness of tone and the breath mechanism. This awareness can be memorised and replicated by the student in the practice room, resulting in consistency in singing instead of the student's attempt to recall images of hot pizza, triangles, pears, and copper wire. Perhaps an approach that involves an instructor explaining and preparing the student for where he or she will physically feel vibration, awareness, or sensation of vocal tone, while addressing the singer holistically, can result in more success. In other words, it may be perhaps most helpful to blend a pedagogical approach based in science and anatomy with clear, concise explanations of sensory awareness with an approach using some imagery to foster expressive singing.

The next section will consider a natural approach to vocal instruction. The natural approach will show tenets similar to those in the French school of thought. There will be little focus placed on the anatomy of the vocal mechanism. As well, in the natural approach there is little instruction on the use of breath support or consideration of placement of the vocal tone.

Natural Approach

An additional category that is used in higher education is the natural approach. This approach is unrelated to a scientific approach but has similar tenets to those found in an approach based in imagery. In a natural pedagogical approach, there is little discussion of the mechanics or physiological aspects of singing. The underpinnings of a natural approach to singing are natural breath, as in speech, singing related to the speaking voice, natural or relaxed posture, and a tension-free body. There is some similarity to a method based in imagery, as students are presented with calming images or are encouraged to dance as a way to engage in natural, tension-free singing. The tenets of an approach in natural instruction parallel much of what was described in the French national school of singing. Breath support is quite natural and speech-like, posture is natural, and much of the focus is placed in text interpretation and poetic imagery.

An instructor using a natural method does not base instruction on the mechanics of singing, as this may cause tension and the natural teacher feels it unnecessary. Fields (1947) states, "Because of the involuntary nature of vocal action it is not necessary for the singer to have knowledge of the structure of his vocal organs in order to govern their action properly" (p. 34). The central tenets of this approach are natural breathing and a natural approach to tone; in other words, the student should not consider tone placement, resonance, or breath support.

The notion of breath support is notable in a natural approach. Several of the instructors reviewed use a natural approach to teaching breath management. One of the male instructors uses an approach of "non-interference" (Blades-Zeller, 2003, p. 84). He attempts to bring students to a "natural poise of balance" before singing (p. 84). This is an attempt to encourage the student to take in breath and sing tension free. Another female instructor says she does not teach breath support and uses an approach similar to the interpretive method focusing on tone and text. She speaks about other aspects of singing and assumes the student will inevitably breathe well. She does not encourage breath support as she feels it may result in pressure and tension. An additional female instructor gives images to encourage natural inhalation; she gives students calming and pleasant images for relaxation or ideas of breathing in colors and filling the body with the warmth of the colors (2003). One of the female instructors surveyed uses a very natural approach to breath instruction. Much of her instruction of breath revolves around movement in the melodic line, with the idea that the breath moves through the music. Another female instructor also uses musical phrases and movement to instruct vocal tone and the feeling of movement in the breath (2003). This approach may not result in a coordinated and consistent singing. Though some students may have natural coordination of the muscles, some training is required. Miller (1986) indicates:

> It may be commendable, if you are a naturally coordinated animal, never giving thought to the breath (you do not think about breath when you are not singing, so why when you sing?) or to any other aspect of singing technique. Inasmuch as singing is a physical as well as artistic act (and part of its artistic strength lies in the physical freedom displayed); the teaching of voice chiefly from the text and the music is mostly inadequate. (p. 210)

The result may be singers who are not creating the full capacity of sound they can make if not using adequate breath support, in other words they will not have the ability to produce a sound that will carry or project. This is similar to the prevalence of lighter voices found in the French national school of singing. If the student uses minimal breath or is taught to breathe as in speaking, this will limit the sound power ratio potential. When a singer finds an optimal resonant singing tone, the amount of breath that is expelled determines how much volume or power he or she will make. If a student wishes to sing as a soloist above an orchestra and choir, for example, it is necessary that he or she know how to use the breath to find a full sound. It is similar to when one strikes the keys of an acoustic piano; if one lightly touches the key, the result will be a light, thin tone. Or if one bows a violin or cello without strength in the bowing arm, the result will be a soft, thin tone. As well, it takes strength to produce a clear tone at low volume, whether singing, playing piano, violin, or cello. There must be energy in the tone.

Several instructors use text, speech, and diction as a natural approach when instructing singing and the release of tension (Blades-Zeller, 2003; Fields, 1947; Miller, 1997). One of the female instructors uses diction as a tool to diagnose and release tension. She encourages stretching, and gives students cues such as telling them to have "peace at the center" (p. 79). One of the males instructs by having students engage in "non-singing sounds" (p. 39). He has students begin with diction— crying certain words, and then eventually connecting the words to sustained singing tones. Another also uses a natural approach of connecting the speaking voice to the singing tone (2003). One of the females uses a pedagogical method that is quite natural. Much focus is placed on interpretation of text, diction, and musicality. She does not address vocal registers, anatomy, or speak of resonant singing tones. This approach can help build artistry and interpretative skills but may need to be balanced with a scientific approach.

Natural singing is also instructed using a rote method involving imitation. Samoiloff (1942), remarks that a voice student "learns best by imitation" (p. 13). In this natural method, the student is instructed to imitate the sound or vocal tone produced by the teacher or from a recording. The student is not instructed as to how to produce the sound, but is asked just to imitate the sound. Samoiloff continues by describing a natural method of instruction involving imagery, and discusses a method that goes beyond the anatomy of singing, stating, "In direct contrast to the mechano-physiological[11] school is that group of teachers who preach the 'natural' method, sometimes dubbed the 'sing-like-the-birdies-sing method'" (p. 12). This method involves thinking of a beautiful tone and then repeating it. Jack Coldiron instructs students to "imagine the most beautiful sound you think you're capable of making, then try it" (Blades-Zeller, 2003, p. 99). This form of imitation may not address the individual singer and her unique tone. If a student is trying to imitate the singing tone of the teacher or others, then he or she is not developing his or her individual sound.

Passion and meditation are also encouraged within a natural approach to instruction. Madeline Bruser (2011) discusses how a teacher can guide the student to passion. "In making music, we mix passion with discipline. Our love for a piece of music motivates us to become intimate with it by producing the sound ourselves, with our instrument and our own body"

(p. 106). Bruser's approach entails freeing the individual from tension through meditation. Although many teachers believe that meditation can instill passion or emotion, Bruser does not clearly present how meditation will help a student to sing technically well.

In the next example, the author suggests modeling passion as a way to instruct. Wurgler writes (1997), "Teachers must feed the passion for singing that brought them into a life in the arts in the first place. They must model that love and share it enthusiastically with others, most importantly, their students" (p. 7)

In a similar perspective to meditation and passion, some instructors use a natural approach involving dancing and drumming as a way to encourage natural movement and release of tension in the singer. Ristad (1982) uses this method in her natural approach to instruction. She uses drumming, improvisation, and dancing as a way for students to find natural posture and release physical, mental, and emotional tension. This method addresses just one aspect of singing, the release of tension, and may not result in a student finding a consistent singing sound and developing the ability to sing in a healthy manner.

Another concept found in a natural approach to instructing voice in higher education institutions is the Alexander Technique®. The Alexander Technique was created by Frederick Matthias Alexander in the 1890s. He created the technique in response to his own vocal health issues and as a result of losing his voice during acting performances. Briefly, the process in the Alexander Technique is to release all muscular tension in the body and to

---

[11] Mechano-physical is a term that Samoiloff uses to describe an approach based in science and vocal anatomy.

align the neck and spine, returning oneself to a natural posture. It uses elements of tension and muscle release combined with natural breathing and balance. The first step is to release tension, the next is to learn new ways of holding oneself, then how to breathe in the most natural manner and, finally, to learn how to physically and mentally react to situations that may cause tension. Higher education voice instructors generally do not teach this technique; however, voice instructors commonly refer many students to Alexander coaches (Alexander, 2001; Blades-Zeller, 2003; Brennan & Marwood, 2004; Miller, 1986, 1997; Morgan, 2010; Jones, 1997). The Alexander Technique is becoming part of the curriculum in many music departments.[12]

Some of the underpinnings in this approach can be beneficial for the voice student. I believe the principles of good posture and tension release and the importance placed on expressiveness are quite positive. There is, however, a concern with such little emphasis on awareness of the vocal mechanism and how it functions, as well as the natural, speech-like approach to instructing breath control. This lack of awareness of how the voice functions and the little emphasis placed on breath support for the fragile vocal mechanism may lead to vocal fatigue, hoarseness, and potential long-term damage (Frederick, 2006; Sataloff, 1998; Teachey, Kahane & Beckford, 1991).

The Feldenkrais Method® may also be considered a natural approach as it was created to return one to a natural posture, and to create awareness of motions or movement that may cause pain or fatigue in the body. The method was created by Dr. Moshé Feldenkrais (1990), as a result of his inability to recover from an injury. Feldenkrais decided to explore the possibilities of approaching his body's reaction to the injury differently. There are two different sources of pain, limitation of movement, and discomfort: physical conditions, as well as unconscious choices one makes in how one moves. It is an experimental method in which the individual engages in self-awareness of how certain movement may affect how one feels. There are two aspects to the Feldenkrais Method: the process of Awareness Through Movement (ATM), which is a guided group session; and Functional Integration (FI), which is a one-on-one hand on session with a Feldenkrais practitioner. Nelson and Blades (2005) explain the five ideas involved in the method: "1) Life as a process, 2) effective movement involves the whole self as necessary for effective movement, 3) learning as the key activity of humans, 4) the necessity of choice, and 5) the logic of human development. That life is a process should be self-evident" (p. 147). When they examined the use of Feldenkrais

---

[12] Acadia University, Boston University, Guildhall School of Music and Drama, The Julliard School, Manhattan School of Music, McGill University, New England Conservatory of Music, University of Toronto and the University of Maryland.

in the voice studio, Dr. Nelson applied hands on FI, and Dr. Blades examined physical issues that students displayed while singing. The Feldenkrais method, as it applies to vocal instruction, appears to have some beneficial elements. Any activity that instills self-awareness in a student can be beneficial for gaining consistency in singing. Awareness of the breath and how it functions, as well as integrating movement that is conducive to better breath control is beneficial for students. As well, the notion of addressing posture and striving for tension-free movement is helpful for singers. The use of the Feldenkrais method in combination with a pedagogical approach involving knowledge and vocal science and anatomy, and the facilitation of an emotional connection to text, perhaps through some use of imagery, may help build consistency and emotional engagement in students.

Singing is far from a natural activity. It is an athletic undertaking. It takes more than a natural approach to manage the onset and release of a supported vocal tone, to maintain good posture, and to be able to change the shape of the vocal tract (through how much the mouth is opened, the palate lifted, and the shape and position of the tongue), which in turn affects the passive resonators located in the throat and chest.

The next section explores what are considered holistic approaches to vocal instruction. These are approaches that proponents claim to address the singer and complete person and incorporate the mind, body, spirit, and experience of the person. As I will describe, considerable focus is placed on the use of breath for relaxation and the release of tension. This approach may not help to mitigate inconsistent singing if it does not also address other aspects of the singer beyond the breath.

Holistic Approach

A holistic outlook is an approach that considers the mind, body, experience, and spirit of the individual. Some attempts have been made to address various aspects of how the vocal mechanism functions as a whole (breath, and resonance); however, in several of the following approaches pedagogues still appear to merely consider a holistic approach as a description of aspects of the vocal mechanism as opposed to a teaching focus in one area such as breath. Other attempts at holism involve offering a stress-free environment in the voice studio as a way to instruct a singer holistically. Further attempts at a holistic approach involve reviewing historic teaching approaches, how the voice functions physically, and advice on business ethics in the voice studio.

Sell (2005) claims that her approach is holistic and that her book is the first to address a comprehensive approach to vocal instruction. The book, however, is quite similar to other texts written in the field of vocal pedagogy (Bunch 1997; Bunch Dayme, 2005; David, 1995; Deere, 2005; Doscher, 1994; Miller, 1986; Miller, 2005; Stark, 1999). Many of these books offer descriptions of the scientific function of the voice: breath, posture, resonance, and laryngeal function. Texts such as Miller's (1986) and Bunch's (1997) offer quite detailed diagrams of the anatomy of the voice, resonators, and the respiratory system as it relates to singing. Sell's (2005) book does not offer as much detail. Her book gives a history of various approaches to vocal instruction; however, others have also presented a concise history (Miller, 1997; Stark, 1999). What her book offers is a comprehensive reference review of part of the history of vocal pedagogy, a brief description that Sell calls the psychology of teaching and ethics, an overview of the anatomy of singing, a discussion of vocal range and classification, and a section on vocal health. The portion of the book that discusses technique reviews various ideas on breath management, vocal onset and offset, and resonance. The description of the psychology of teaching briefly describes cognitive and developmental psychology; consequently, it describes how a teacher should have a teaching plan and a systematic plan to achieve the teaching outcome. Though it is important to have a goal for each student, there must be flexibility and freedom in the pedagogical approach. The book also offers business management advice for teachers and offer tips for students in performance (ideas such as bringing money for the parking meter). Sell's (2005) approach to vocal pedagogy does offer a comprehensive review of various aspects of singing, but it does not consider the student holistically, as an individual made up of a body, mind, and soul. The book does not offer concrete ideas of how to translate the knowledge of vocal anatomy and technique to the student. It would seem apparent that this approach is not holistic and may not facilitate consistency in singing, an emotional connection to music for the students, nor an opportunity for a teacher and student to explore freedom in their facilitative relationship.

Smith (2007) presents a book with ideas that appear to have a more well-rounded approach to singing than Sell's (2005), although it does not offer ideas on how to instruct a student using his pedagogical method. The book is designed as a self-study for singers, with some standardised exercises and a CD. In this sense, it does not align with a completely holistic approach based in the idea of freedom in existentialist terms. There is little room to explore the student-teacher relationship and the approach does not appear to contain much flexibility in instruction. It is a positive example of an approach that looks at almost all of the makeup of a singer. The author describes the breath mechanism, posture, and alignment. His technique is comprised of what he calls inventions (such as the piano inventions or studies of J. S. Bach). These are divided into six sections: (a) speaking (b) free-flowing air (c) balancing act (d) spontaneous combustion (e) the wobble and (f) getting high. The first invention speaks of linking the singing voice to speech. He does not, however, elaborate on the concept of resonance or how a singer can find a resonant singing tone consistently. He does not offer suggestions as to how to obtain kinesthetic awareness of the vocal tone. It appears that by using his speech to singing exercises to strengthen intrinsic and extrinsic muscles of the vocal folds, the singer will find a singing tone. The next invention gives ideas and exercises on breath support for the voice.

Smith's descriptions do give a clear picture of how the breath mechanism functions in singing. The balancing act portion gives exercises and ideas of how to balance the voice through the low, middle, and high registers. His descriptions are concise in this section of the book. The following invention gives exercises for the onset and release of the vocal tone; in other words, how to begin a vocal tone/line and how to conclude a vocal tone/line. His description is clear in this regard as well. The wobble invention gives exercises on how to build agility and flexibility in the voice, and the final invention presents exercises that work the entire vocal range from bottom to top. The technical exercises in this portion of the book give clear descriptions; however, they are quite prescriptive. Without the author addressing the student-teacher relationship and how the teacher may facilitate these ideas, the outcome may not be consistency in singing.

There is a beneficial portion of Smith's book that offers advice to the singer on having good diction and musicianship, on working on agility of the voice, and how to approach different musical styles. He suggests that the singer pick appropriate repertoire for herself. He also gives pointers on good audition techniques, steps for learning repertoire, financial management, preparedness, how to work with conductors/directors, good vocal health, and lifestyle. These are important aspects, and they offer a glimpse of the entire singer. The book does not appear beneficial to the pre-service or higher education instructor, in that it does not appear to suggest ways to facilitate this information for students. His approach does not appear to be flexible and individualised, and there seems to be an assumption that if a singer uses Smith's exercises, she will sing well. The student-teacher relationship in the voice studio must be facilitated by a teacher with a varied set of teaching tenets and with the ability to translate these ideas in a flexible way, depending on how the voice is functioning and developing, as well as in a manner that is of benefit to the individual student. There must be freedom in the relationship between the student and teacher.

Additionally, Smith does not engage in any discussion of emotions or aesthetics in music or performance. Given that his ideas are intended to build vocal technique in a student, a truly holistic approach to teaching the individual should include exploring the spirit, mind, or experience of the student engaged in voice study and during performance.

Smith's ideas may be of benefit to a teacher with a great deal of experience and a successful method of communication with her students, in that she will be able to interpret his ideas and explain them to her students if she wishes to explore other approaches.

Another method that can be considered holistic is that of Elliot (2010). She uses an approach based in the Buddhist meditation called *Vipassana* in her vocal instruction at Princeton University. The approach is based in meditative breathing and the Mindful Based Stress Reduction Method (MBSRD). The intent is to use the breath to relax the student's posture and deepen breath so as to calm the singer, ease nervousness, alleviate self-doubt, and help the student stay in the present moment while singing. Though deep breathing is essential as a part of good vocal technique, it is not apparent how focusing on one aspect of vocal technique—the breath— will help a singer develop her instrument fully. It is beneficial for a singer to remain calm and to take low breaths to support the sound; however, an approach based in meditation and awareness of deep breathing is not enough to facilitate vocal development. An approach such as this does not address how the vocal mechanism functions in its complete form, combining the use of breath as well as resonance, posture, articulation, and an emotional connection to text and music.

A female voice instructor (2013) indicates how she instructed holistic voice lessons in a manner defined as "A Body, Mind, Spirit Approach to Singing with Freedom and Authenticity." [13] Her approach is based in yoga and meditation. This approach appears to parallel tenets of the natural approach such as those described in the previous section as used by Bruser (2011) and of the Mindful Based Stress Reduction Method (MBSRD) that influenced Elliott (2010). Rose was contacted to clarify her use of the term "freedom" as it applies to singing; however, she did not respond.

Additional holistic voice instructors such as Karen Lyu (2013), Irene Mastrangeli, (2013), Jessie Richards (2013), Heidi Siegell (2013), Sounding Circles (2013), and Anita Suhanin (2013) teach with what they call a holistic method of vocal instruction. The focus of the instruction appears to be centered in meditation, breathing, calming of mind and spirit, and building confidence through meditation to uncover what is the source of mental and physical tension.

The Royans Professional Vocal School (2013) offers a Vocal Science Program®. This program's description is quite misleading, as it claims to be both holistic and scientific at the same time. This program will be described in more detail in the contemporary methods section; however, it is mentioned in this section as it self-defines as a holistic approach. The Vocal Science Program® will be considered in the contemporary section, as this section will describe methods created within the past fifty years.

---

[13] Description of the nature of Ms. Rose's lessons are found on her website: www.holisticlessons.com

There is an institution of holistic higher education that offers a holistic music degree. The Maharishi University of Management (2013) offers courses that are instructed so that students have a holistic experience in music education. There are voice lessons provided, as well lessons in as other instruments in this program of study. The course descriptions, however, do not include the pedagogical approach used in vocal instruction.

Some of the approaches considered holistic exhibit parallels to the natural approach with regard to the release of tension in the body. The holistic outlook does provide deeper physical awareness of the breath and relaxation, which can help students. A student with a tension-free body, calm mind, and who can access deep breath will be closer to a path of consistency in singing than a student who is not instructed or guided to sing tension free with awareness of the breath.

Some instructors may be reluctant to engage in self-reflection or may not wish to consider incorporating other pedagogical approaches, such as the methods described in this section, in addition to what they currently use. This reluctance can contribute to furthering the problem of inconsistent singing. Bunch Dayme (2006) notes that many voice professionals have not explored approaches or recommended ideas based in Eastern practice such as Tai Chi, yoga, or mediation. She suggests, "Perhaps one reason is that the practitioners do little in the avenue of self-development" (p. 62).

The holistic approaches described in this section vary in emphasis and in how to apply their principles when instructing voice. These discrepancies are similar to those illustrated in the teaching approaches based in imagery and imagination and in the natural approach. There is confusion about what constitutes a holistic pedagogical approach in vocal instruction. A holistic approach is said to consider the whole student. If this is so, it should address each aspect of the student and not just breath, for example. Some approaches may offer what is considered a whole overview of voice study; however, these ideas neglect to address the student-teacher relationship and how the teacher may facilitate this information for the student.

The pedagogical methods reviewed in this section according to the definition of holism should offer a complete idea of how to instruct the whole student (mind, body, spirit, and experience), or explore the student-teacher relationship with teacher as facilitator; ironically, this is not apparent. Offering a stress-free environment for study may help a student remain calm, but it will not help a student gain vocal consistency, nor will writing a description of the function of the voice without consideration of how to relay this information to the student be helpful. The various ideas of holism may further inconsistency and confusion for a higher education student engaged in voice study.

A truly holistic vocal instructor must have complete knowledge of how the voice functions (science and anatomy). The holistic teacher must also have in his or her set of teaching tools knowledge of anatomy and an ability to guide the student to make a connection as to how the anatomy functions as it relates to singing. As well, he or she must have flexibility and the ability to use any individualised combination of vocal science, imagery, imagination, a natural or tension-free approach, as well as incorporating aspects of contemporary approaches, defined in the next section.

The next section presents another category of vocal instruction. This category describes contemporary approaches to music and vocal instruction. These methods are considered some of the more contemporary approaches to singing, as they were created in the last fifty years. As well, some of these approaches are used as a way to instruct what is considered contemporary music (musical theatre, jazz, or pop). Some of the methods have parallels to the holistic methods, in that they attempt to view the singer as an entire being, and some have foundations in breath and posture management.

Contemporary Approaches

This section will outline additional methods of vocal pedagogy that may be considered contemporary, as they were developed within the last fifty years. To this day, there is still little research in this area. There are several schools of thought for this genre, but the world of contemporary commercial study even in 2020 is highly under-researched. Some of the approaches have tenets with a foundation similar to some of the holistic approaches based in meditative breathing and posture alignment, and some have a focus on the use of the speaking voice. This may present some ambiguity in teaching approaches and confusion by overlapping styles that are more suited to musical theatre or other more popular music with the classical genre. This can cause some vocal health issues for students if attempted for use in classical repertoire. If a student is approaching the singing of classical repertoire with a teaching method based in the use of the speaking voice (with a great deal of low or chest resonance) with breath support one would use for the speaking voice, this may cause vocal strain and fatigue and an inability to project the voice. Some of the newer approaches build their foundation from what is called speech level singing. This is a controversial method in the field of classical singing, as it appears to focus primarily on connecting the speaking voice to the singing voice without much consideration of the breath support required to support the singing voice. It is not an approach that should be taken without having the guidance of a knowledgeable contemporary vocal instructor. Some instructors examined in this section appear to make some use of speech level singing in higher education voice studios, but combine it with breath support (Smith, 2007).

Many of the contemporary methods that will be described make the claim that a contemporary method is the only way to sing in a healthy manner. Some will claim that voices can be repaired or that one can be taught to become "a star" in 10 lessons. These claims will be detailed further in each method's description; however, it is clear that such claims and statements can be detrimental to the perception of the validity of a method. Many of the contemporary methods that will be examined make use of the internet and websites, videos, and CD training as a way to translate information about their methods, instead of using printed material and textbooks. This is perhaps another characteristic of contemporary approaches to instruction. Some teachers also offer lessons via Skype®.

The first contemporary method to be discussed is Somatic Voicework™, The LoVetri method. This method is considered useful for contemporary styles of music such as musical theatre, pop, and folk music. However, this method is used in some higher education institution voice studios.[14] The claim made by LoVetri (Woodruff, 2011) is that her method is an appropriate style for classical singers, although it is considered a method for the singing of commercial contemporary music: musical theatre, belting, rock, or gospel (LoVetri, 2008). Proponents of the LoVetri approach contend that it is an effective method for college voice faculty given its systematic exercise, which can be easily blended into a current teaching philosophy.[15] Despite these claims, there is little evidence that suggests that this approach is effective for vocal instruction of classical repertoire though beneficial for the instruction of contemporary commercial music. Reviews of the principles of the method show that its foundations are based in proper alignment, strengthening the upper body and abdominal muscles, and the principle that as the body strengthens so does the voice. Other ideas mentioned are that each person is always doing his or her own best, the singer always knows best, and the body has its own wisdom and always goes towards health.[16] The first principles align with other methods that encourage good posture and strength in the abdominal muscles (which in turn should help promote good breath support). These ideas appear to promote good vocal technique. The other ideas, including that each person is always doing her best, that the singer always knows best, and that the body has its own wisdom do not align with a pedagogical method that promotes facilitation of vocal consistency. Each singer may not always do her best. As well, the singer may not know what is best and the body may not have its own wisdom. If this were the case, why would one need to engage in a course of vocal study by this method or any other? The statements may cause confusion as to why one engages in vocal study. A student must be guided and facilitated through building a vocal technique to encourage healthy vocal development leading to consistency in

---

[14] Dalhousie University, Shenandoah Conservatory, and the University of Central Oklahoma.
[15] http://www.somaticvoicework.com/
[16] http://somaticvoicework.com/somatic-voicework-core-principles.aspx

singing. The method does encourage the expression of emotions through music. While this may be advantageous at first glance, if one is distracted by a lack of knowledge of breath support appropriate to the respective style of vocal repertoire, the student may to attempt to push the voice so that he or she can attempt to express the desired emotions in singing through overexerting. The emotional energy is misguided.

Pushing the voice is an approach predominantly used by singers of rock or pop music, in which there is not a great deal of emphasis placed on the use of natural resonance and projection of the voice through breath support. It is further notable that little importance is placed on vocal health. A strong body and awareness of the body is beneficial for vocal development. It must, however, be in combination with instruction as to how the voice functions scientifically. As well, instruction should be combined with an awareness of posture and alignment and function of the breath mechanism, and it must encourage musicianship and individualised emotional connection to music and text. This method does not appear to facilitate individualised instruction. It does promote the idea of each voice being as unique as a fingerprint; however, a set of prescriptive exercises may not help the student develop her individual sound or consistency in singing. There is a great deal of inconsistency in how the LoVetri method is self-defined. In one aspect, the approach is considered systematic, with sets of exercises gauged towards vocal function; however, the method is also intended to be individualised. It is not clear how a teacher can address the student with individualised instruction by using a set of systematic exercises. This is a contradiction that may leave a student confused about how to approach vocal development and that will further inconsistent singing.

The next group of pedagogical methods or schools of thought stem from the use of speech and the speaking voice as the foundation of a vocal technique. These are Speech Level Singing™, Estill Voice Training™, and Complete Vocal Technique of the Complete Vocal Institute. As will be discussed, many of these methods appear to be corporations that are selling systematic approaches to vocal instruction and addressing one aspect of the singer and vocal study.

Speech Level Singing™ was created by voice instructor, a Hollywood vocal coach.[17] The method claims to be beneficial to all singers from opera to rock. Briefly, this technique requires that the larynx stay low and then raises it to produce upper notes with what is called a "twang." One can imagine the nasal twang that a country or some musical theatre performers use in the upper register if one attempts to place the voice in the nasal passage and streamlines the color with little volume. There is little to no importance placed on instructing breath support, vowel and vocal tract shaping, or resonance and

---

[17] http://www.sethriggs.com/

how the voice may be naturally amplified by accessing the resonating cavities. The approach starts with notes in the lower register, indicating that a great deal of volume or drive should be placed on these speech level notes. The middle voice is to be modified or streamlined, and the upper range is approached by "twanging" notes— in other words placing the voice in the nasal passages. The approach is systematic and formulaic: pre-determined exercises are meant to be repeated, and if they don't work, students are instructed to repeat them again.

Riggs (2007), when asked about the importance of teaching breath technique and resonance, replied, "Breathing is a by-product of good technique —just like one's resonance quality is a by-product. You should never work directly at developing your breath unless you have a sloppy posture and a depressed rib cage" (p. 1). This statement is disconcerting. Good vocal technique is an ability to support the vocal folds with sufficient breath management, while allowing the vocal tones to resonate in various resonating chambers in the body, keeping the body and larynx tension free and aligned well. These principles simply <u>must</u> be instructed. It is unclear what Riggs means by technique if he is making an assumption that breath support and resonance are by-products of good technique. Riggs states further, "When you use a speech-level approach to singing, everything, including how much air you use to move your cords, happens automatically" (p.1). This approach may result in a great deal of vocal fatigue, misuse, or perhaps even more detrimental side effects. It would seem quite impossible for a vocal student to automatically obtain good breath support and proper vocal resonance by merely changing the color of the vocal tone as previously described. Without sufficient breath support and an awareness of the requirement of driving the voice in the lower register, the long-term side effects could be detrimental to the vocal health and vocal longevity of a student.

The method appears to be strictly rote exercises, and all instructors use the same ones. There is also a self-study book, *singing for the Stars*, that includes CDs on how to train oneself to sing using this method. The use of a self-study book and CD will not facilitate individualised vocal instruction. A student left to study vocal development on his or her own may sing inconsistently and may also not have the opportunity to explore expressive singing.

This technique has many parallels to the French national school of singing as well as the natural pedagogical approach. Similar to those following the French and natural methods, a singer may not develop the voice to its full potential, since he or she lacks awareness and instruction of correct breath support and proper tension-free transitioning from one vocal register to the next. It appears many pop, rock, and television celebrities use this method of training, although Riggs (2007) states that it is an appropriate technique for opera singers and that its foundations are influenced by classical baritone and tenor singers. As well, the systematic approach or use of repetitive exercises does not offer a student individualised instruction in a flexible environment. The method also offers a self-study book for individuals wishing to learn this technique on their own. A self-study book of vocal technique is not a preferred approach to use, and it is potentially dangerous for a student to engage in such exercises as this method requires. Unsupervised singing of such strenuous exercises requiring a great deal of control and manipulation of vocal mechanism may cause a student to sustain fatigue and may potentially damage the fragile vocal folds and mechanism. Perhaps consideration of a method influenced by existentialist principles with a combination of various methods, flexibility, and the exploration of individual freedom and responsibility may be a more beneficial and a healthier approach for students interested in developing the voice to perform classical repertoire.

Estill Voice Training™ is another method that makes use of the speaking voice and movement through the vocal registers.[18] The process in this method involves a deconstruction of the various structures of singing in order to rebuild these structures in an attempt to gain control over each. In this method, six qualities of singing exist: speech, falsetto, sob, twang, opera, and belt. The method uses instruction based in knowledge of the anatomy of the voice. The creator has engaged in some research of the anatomy of the voice (Colton and Estill, 1981; Honda, Hirai, Estill and Takhura, 1994; Kmucha, Yanagisawa and Estill, 1990; Yanagisawa, Estill, Kmucha and Leder, 1989). The approach uses systematic exercises, or "figures" as they are called in this method, to control thirteen vocal structures:

- true vocal folds
- onset and offset control
- body-cover control
- false vocal folds control
- thyroid cartilage control
- cricoid cartilage control
- larynx control
- velum control
- tongue control
- aryepiglottic sphincter control
- jaw control
- torso control
- lips control

---

[18] http://www.estillvoice.com/pages/about-estill-voice

- head and neck control[19]

The student is instructed to gain awareness of how these structures function. This method has generally been associated with musical theatre and popular styles of music, and it is potentially of benefit to opera singers since through it they could gain awareness of the structures of singing (Estill, 2020). Instructors of this method also employ software: namely, Estill Voiceprint Plus™. This is a voice spectrograph apparatus that teachers may use in the voice studio. In order to teach this method as a certified teacher, one must register for courses and workshops given by Estill Voice International and attain a certain level of certification and proficiency in the use of the Estill Voiceprint program, as well as mastering course manuals for instruction of the various figures as described in the previous paragraphs. All course manuals, software, CDs, and merchandise such as t-shirts, bags, and mugs are purchased through the Estill website, which includes a corporate call center.[20] There are several higher education institutions[21] in the United States and the United Kingdom that offer Estill Voice Training™.

The concept of deconstructing the voice has parallels to the *Stimmbildung* in the German school of singing, which considered breaking apart the components of the voice and then rebuilding them as a beneficial approach (Lehmann, 1993). Though the Estill method may be of benefit for instructors and students in that it encourages awareness of the vocal mechanism and how it functions in contemporary singing, this method of deconstructing and then reconstructing is compartmentalised, focusing on just one aspect of the singer. It is unlikely that a student will gain consistency in singing or an ability to engage emotionally to music and text if instructed with this approach, although they may gain an awareness of the anatomy of the voice. This method appears to have the marketing of the method as part of the focus, as opposed to a humanistic outlook on instructing the individual student to teach her to reach her potential as a singer.

The next contemporary method that makes use of the speaking voice using a predominant chest belt is the Complete Vocal Technique of the Complete Vocal Institute, created by a Danish teacher (1991). She claims that her method is based on physiological information and not myths, and that it is a way to sing in a healthy manner. All singers should be able to apply the method immediately; if not, Sadolin says that the singer is doing something wrong (1991).

---

[19] These elements are the anatomical structures that make up the vocal mechanism. In this method the student is instructed on how to attempt to isolate these structures.
[20] http://www.estillvoice.com/
[21] Motherwell College, Mars Hill College, and University of Central Florida.

The three principles of the method start with the idea that there should be support for the voice. This aligns with traditional bel canto technique. The next principle indicates that there should be a certain amount of twang (or sharpness) in the sound. Sadolin (2000) defines twang as a sharp piercing sound. This twang is created by closing down and reducing the size of the epiglottis funnel (area above the vocal folds resulting in a tone with clarity). As a long-time vocal instructor, I believe that constricting or intentionally trying to produce a sharp piercing tone raises concerns as to the benefit of this method – this appears to be about restriction and constriction which should not be incorporated in any method of vocal instruction. The next principle indicates that there should be no tension in the jaw or lips and that the jaw should not protrude while singing, as this may cause tension. This is a beneficial principle for singing. One should attempt to sing with as little tension as possible. This idea, however, appears to contradict the idea of twanging, as this sound is created by constricting space in the area above the vocal folds.

Using this method, singing is approached in four modes: (a) neutral (b) curbing (c) overdrive and (d) edge (2000). Each one is defined by the amount of "metal" in the sound. It is not traditional or, frankly, encouraging to describe the vocal tone as metallic. It offers an image of a vocal tone or quality that is cold, harsh, and hard somehow. The method, however, describes the mode as neutral in which there is no metal in the sound. This mode is to be used when one is singing softly or in pop music when one desires a breathy tone. The next mode is described as curbing the tone. This entails bringing a certain amount of metal to the vocal tone while restricting, or having a moaning, wailing, or whining quality. It is indicated that one should restrict or curb one's sound in this mode. The next mode is called overdrive. This mode is described as similar to shouting, as when one calls out to someone on the street hoping to get her attention. This mode is to contain a great deal of metal in the tone. In pop music, it is to be used in loud passages, and is rarely used in classical repertoire. The last mode is called edge. This tone is to contain a great deal of metal or a full-metallic mode. There is a significant idea of twang used in this tone. It is described as aggressive and screaming. Sadolin (2000) describes this tone as one imitating a diving airplane.

When the singer is aware of the principles and modes, she is able to apply them using a light or dark vocal tone. The singer also has options to choose vocal effects such as grunt, rattle, or creak, for example. A summary of the technique is represented in Diagram 2 (Sadolin, 2000).

3 overall principles	• support • necessary twang • Avoid protruding the jaw and tightening the lips

CHOOSE VOCAL MODE

NEUTRAL

CURBING

OVERDRIVE

EDGE

CHOOSE SOUND COLOUR

DARK   **LIGHT**

PERHAPS CHOOSE EFFECT

- distortion
- creak and creaking
- rattle
- growl
- grunt
- screams
- vocal breaks
- air added to the voice
- vibrato
- techniques for ornamentation

Some of the principles, modes and effects described in this technique appear to put a great deal of strain on the fragile vocal mechanism. The average adult vocal folds are just slightly larger than the thumbnail (Gray, 2000). Striving for sounds that appear to be made by constricting the area above the vocal folds as well as attempting to incorporate a metallic quality to the voice may result in discomfort for a singer. In addition, naming vocal modes with words like curb, edge, or overdrive may cause singers or teachers considering this method to worry about vocal health. The book describing the Complete Vocal Method also comes with a CD and scripted vocal exercises. This does not represent a pedagogical method that is individualised. All singers may not have the same level of vocal development, and it is more beneficial to work with each student individually without scripted exercises that one must repeat over and over again. It is also disconcerting to envision a student working with a book and CD without supervision, trying to implement a metallic quality to her tone or attempting to create effects such as growl, grunt, or scream without a knowledgeable teacher present to ensure vocal health.

Sadolin's (2000) chapters describing her method give a great deal of information on the anatomy of the voice. There are detailed diagrams and descriptions of breath mechanisms, as well as the anatomy of the vocal tract and throat. This may be of benefit to a teacher or student who wishes to gain scientific knowledge of the anatomy of the vocal mechanism and its components; however, it does not appear to be a method that will help a student gain consistency in singing. It may be beneficial for pop or rock singers, who may not have as much concern with long term vocal health or singing using natural resonance—in other words, without amplification. Sadolin does indicate her method may be used in all genres of singing including classical repertoire, but many of the modes— including curbing, overdrive, and, in particular, edge —do not align well with classical singing.

Critique on Current Schools of Thought

These pedagogical approaches represent the varied ways voice is currently instructed in higher education music institutions. Current methods of vocal instruction find their historic roots in the German, French, Italian, and English traditions of instruction. For a student of vocal pedagogy, a new voice instructor, or currently practicing voice instructor in higher education, these national categories are quite broad and present challenges in finding a pedagogical method that he or she may use. Specifically, they do not address ways to approach aspects of the instruction of vocal technique, but rather provide an overview of a traditional approach to singing, or a desired sound or posture, for example. A new voice teacher may not find using an approach from the European tradition beneficial for instruction in North American higher education institutions. It is important, however, for students and teachers to be aware of these national traditions that have influenced current pedagogy.

Instructional models based in vocal science and anatomy, imagery and imagination, natural approaches, and holistic and contemporary approaches were examined for this research study. Some of these models of instruction have limitations and may be considered to address just one aspect of instruction and not take the entire singer into consideration. Focusing on just one aspect on instruction will not give the student or teacher access to what he or she can truly become as a teacher or as a student. A teacher who is exposed to and well versed in numerous approaches has the ability to choose from his or her skill set to find the best method to instruct each student as an individual. This instructor will have the ability to be a flexible facilitator of vocal technique, addressing each student's different needs. In having the ability to utilize a varied skill set, the teacher is not limited, and thus the student benefits from this knowledge. The teacher must first facilitate vocal technique using a varied, individualised and flexible approach so that the student sings consistently and has the ability to be expressive.

There cannot be a standardized or set approach to vocal instruction, given that each student and voice is unique and must be approached in various ways. A scientific approach, for example, appears quite prescriptive, in that each student may be given the same set of standardized exercises without addressing her individual needs. Equally, a pedagogy based solely in imagery is too ambiguous, and a natural approach may leave the student lacking full vocal development. If the student is not using adequate breath support, for example, she may not develop her full vocal sound and may encounter vocal health issues. Singing is an athletic activity that requires management of the respiratory system. If one considers a holistic approach, it should address all aspects of the individual mind, body, spirit, and emotions. The holistic approaches examined for this study did not appear to address the entire singer and focused on just one aspect: breath, or release of tension, for example. In this study, I am not suggesting that these approaches cannot provide some benefit to students in vocal development, but rather I wish to present a way to look at some guiding principles of vocal instruction that use a broad spectrum of the presented approaches in a fluid and flexible manner and attempt to mitigate inconsistent and unemotional singing.

The student-teacher relationship in the voice studio should involve the teacher facilitating good vocal technique, awareness of the instrument and how it functions scientifically, and good vocal health. This can be attempted by using a balanced approach to ensure the student is able to sing technically correctly and consistently while remaining aware of vocal health. The teacher must, however, also foster an experience of joy and artistic interpretation in singing to keep this important live art form relevant in a culture where so much is manufactured and created artificially. Some use of imagery for engaging the emotions of the student in a song or text can be helpful in guiding emotional experience. Instruction using some of the tenets of tension-free singing in the natural approach can be helpful for a student to release tension in the body and vocal tone.

The limitation that these varied approaches have is that the teacher is not instructing the student as a complete singer, both as a technically proficient musician and an artist, but rather is appearing to offer compartmentalised instruction of just certain aspects of singing. A gap exists in these approaches. Many of the methods examined focus on just the technical aspects of singing; specifically, finding a way to produce a good vocal tone. Some teaching methods examined, such as those based in science and anatomy, attempt to help build technical proficiency through scientific awareness of how the voice functions. These methods may be helpful in building consistency in singing but are lacking in helping to engage emotions. Others attempt to help the student sing in a desired way through the use of imagery as a means to find his or her singing tone. This may help the student find a clear and released tone during a lesson, but may present a challenge for the student to reproduce in a practice room. The natural approach may consistent of encouraging the student to "do nothing," as was discussed in the French tradition, or may focus on relaxation. The holistic methods attempt to help the student release tension in the body and voice, while some of the contemporary methods appear more suited to the singing of pop and rock and are not conducive to the singing that is studied at most higher education voice departments. These methods attempt to teach consistency in singing. As argued in the previous sections, many pedagogical approaches address just one aspect of singing and may not all help foster consistency. These methods fail to consider the complete singer as an artist who is capable of exploring choice and artistic freedom of expression.

Using a balanced, truly holistic approach to vocal instruction, the teacher will consider the singer as a complete person, as a human being capable of making artistic choices. An all-encompassing method may provide students with knowledge and awareness of how to sing consistently, as well guide them to explore artistic choice, thus giving them an opportunity to emotionally engage during performance in this unique art form.

Conclusion

The voice teacher's goal is fostering the student to become an artist, to reach a level of technical proficiency and independence so that he or she can make artistic choices in performance. Many methods attempt to encourage a student to make a desired vocal tone through the use of vocal science, through imagery or imagination, through meditation, or through the use of singing related to speech. These methods leave a gap and appear not to help mitigate inconsistent singing. As well, they fall short in fostering emotions and artistic choice in performance.

The source of inconsistent and emotionally unengaged singing, I believe, is the teacher, and how he or she is instructing the student. What is not being explored in these pedagogical methods is the facilitative relationship between a teacher and student, the role of the teacher, and how effective he or she is in this relationship. Teachers do not usually address or consider how they relate to students (Brown, 2000).

With certain teaching approaches, such as those based in imagery, natural approaches, holistic approaches, and some based in science and anatomy, the burden appears to be on the student to produce a desired vocal tone. What must be examined is the teacher: how the teacher has a responsibility; and can have the ability to choose from a varied set of teaching tools to help foster consistency and independence in singing. This is done through guidance, and through not leaving the student to find this consistency alone. An exploration of the role of the teacher will examine how the teacher can instruct and guide the student to find consistency and artistry in singing.

In both the technical and natural approaches to singing, the role of the teacher is not sufficiently examined. The goal as voice instructors is to instruct singers to become independent artists. Students, however, must be guided to find a level of technical consistency and artistic choice in order to experience this independence and ability to make choices. These teaching approaches lack an articulation or development of how to translate information to the voice student. There must be an articulation of a teaching method, in which the teacher can choose a flexible approach to vocal instruction encompassing any of the varied methods described, depending on the situation presented in each lesson and the individualised student's needs. There must be a student-teacher relationship based in freedom of choice, both for the teacher and student. The teacher can choose any number of approaches to help the student make a connection to technically proficient singing. An all-encompassing approach can help facilitate consistent singing. Using this approach, the teacher guides the student to take responsibility and an active role in the facilitated relationship. The student is not left to mitigate the murky waters of technically proficient singing alone. The student who has consistency in singing can be guided to have artistic freedom and to make choices leading to emotionally engaged performances. As well, a relationship that is based in responsibility can be considered. The teacher is responsible for helping the student make connections to gain consistency in singing. The student can be made aware of his or her responsibility in the learning process and take an active role in building this consistency, thus making artistic choices.

In this research study, I will look at ways to reconsider and reframe how we think about vocal instruction and the student-teacher relationship in the voice studio. I will present principles that have been underexplored in the application of vocal instruction. In the next chapters, I will introduce the consideration and use of several existentialist principles such as freedom, responsibility, anguish, and abandonment and argue how these may be applied to vocal instruction.

CHAPTER 3

Building the Student-Teacher Relationship

INTRODUCTION

The relationship of the student and teacher in vocal instruction are arguably not fully addressed in current teaching methods. After examining the limitations presented in the various teaching approaches, I will consider some of the theoretical principles of existentialism as an approach to address these limitations.

Some existentialist principles have been considered in the student-teacher relationship in an application to general education but have not yet been considered in an application to vocal instruction. This presents an opportunity to expand how faculty approach vocal instruction and pedagogy. Drawing upon some of the key principles of existentialism, I consider how inconsistent and unemotional singing may be repositioned. This theoretical lens provides the foundation upon which to consider how these principles highlight certain underdeveloped aspects of vocal instruction in the student-teacher relationship in higher education. Specifically, I will introduce several existentialist principles of Sartre including *existence, essence, freedom,* and *responsibility,* as well as the *anguish* and *abandonment* that at times stem from the realization of freedom and responsibility. In discussing these tenets of Sartre's existentialist thinking and those stemming from them, I examine how these principles may be considered and may be relevant to how vocal instructors can better facilitate consistent and emotionally engaged singing.

THE EXISTENTIAL PHILOSOPHY OF JEAN-PAUL SARTRE

My initial exploration of existentialist principles drew me in particular to Sartre, to his ideas based in freedom and responsibility and to what extent they could be applied to a teaching approach for vocal instruction. There are many existentialists and "there is no set of problems addressed by all and only those thinkers labelled existentialist" (Sartre, 2001, p. 22). Overlap exists in existentialist thinking; however, various views on existence, the self, free will, and choice influenced my decision to select Sartre as my focus for the purpose of this study.

Existentialist thought centers on the existing individual finding her essence. There are several common themes and views of the individual in existentialist thought as well as some divisions of thought, which I will outline. The notions of free will, choice, and the individual's ability to decide her outcome are frequently found in existentialist writing (Earnshaw, 2006). Existentialism is a view of how the individual can define herself. It is a person-centered philosophy in that it is focused on the individual and an account of the human condition.

Existentialism presents the opportunity to question who we are, what type of life we will we live, and how we will live it. The notion of "being" is important in existentialism. There are various thoughts surrounding this concept. Heidegger, for example, views being and existence as one having potential, whereas Sartre views it as the individual's freedom to be what she desires to be and, in that sense, appears more proactive (Marino, 2004). The individual has control of what she will be become (Marino, 2004). Sartre's existentialism not only describes the idea of being a human (existing), but also promotes the idea of individual freedom. This is extremely important to a singer and performer, in terms of how she produces a sound and interprets a piece of music. An instructor who can facilitate awareness of healthy vocal technique, choices, freedom, independence, and autonomy through existentialist principles may have the possibility of helping a singer become better connected to the text and music, so that she can experience freedom in artistry. In this sense, Sartre's view complements voice study, as the voice student can be given the opportunity to be what she desires to be as a singer. Jaspers (1970) writes of the self, will, and freedom in terms of knowledge and ideas. He says that "whatever exists or occurs is unfree" (p. 155) and that "knowledge does not make me free as yet, but without knowledge there is no freedom" (p. 156). In a Sartrean view of vocal study, unlike Jaspers' thoughts, knowledge can help make one free. If one has knowledge of how to sing consistently, one may experience freedom in singing, freedom from tension, and artistic freedom. Nietzsche's view of the self appears to have an emphasis on the physical body, whereas other existentialist thinkers, such as Sartre, have views that surround consciousness or awareness of the self (Earnshaw, 2006). Consciousness and awareness are important aspects of singing. I believe that the self and one's view on freedom is a perception, a consciousness or awareness. For a voice student, this awareness is essential to her becoming what she desires to be as a singer, regardless of knowledge. An instructor, who can facilitate awareness of healthy vocal technique through instilling responsibility, as well as choices, freedom, and autonomy through existentialist principles, may have the possibility of helping a singer become so connected to the text and music that she can experience freedom in her artistry. The opportunity to explore Sartre's principles further and to consider how they may positively affect consistency and emotional engagement for singers presents a way of changing the way vocal instruction is viewed.

Other divisions are found in existentialist thinking. Within these divisions, one finds Kierkegaard, a theological existentialist, Nietzsche, an anti-Christian existentialist, and Sartre, an atheist existentialist (Marino, 2004). Existentialist views based in theology or atheism also present varied outlooks on being, existence, free will, and choice, and my understanding of these influenced my decision to select Sartre for this study. Kierkegaard, although he writes of free will and choice, defines finding one's authentic self or freedom in a religious context. There is a process of becoming; however, it is defined in theological terms and pre-determined, particularly when he speaks of spheres of existence (Earnshaw, 2006). Kierkegaard believes there are three spheres or three divisions and stages of existence in life: the aesthetic, the ethical, and the religious. These divisions, spheres, or stages are experienced or passed through in order of importance, as one strives towards the highest level of religion. For the individual, Kierkegaard believes one moves from the aesthetic stage, which he classifies as the stage of the "seducer" (p. 31), to the stage or sphere of the ethical, in which he believes one might make a serious commitment such as marriage—a stage in which the individual strives towards living a good life. The individual finally reaches the highest sphere, in which one receives him or herself in the religious sphere. I do not believe that these ideas of spheres or those that Kierkegaard speaks of in his views of existence and being in stages align with my study of an existentialist framework for vocal instruction. I believe that a singer, and what she can become, is not pre-determined, and I do not believe that a singer passes through an aesthetic, ethical, or religious sphere.

Nietzsche and Sartre differ in their views of free will and existence, although they do not take a theological view of existentialism, as Kierkegaard appears to do. Nietzsche speaks of free will and freedom as conquering fate or the set of circumstances we were born into, and of one's striving towards the authentic self. Sartre views the individual as not pre-determined and without fate or circumstances; man, simply is (Marino, 2004, Earnshaw, 2006; Sartre, 2001, 2007). Sartre (2007) writes, "Prior to the projection of the self, nothing exists" (p. 23). For the purpose of this study, Sartre's view is more applicable. Although a voice student has a background prior to entering university, that is her past and, in Sartrean terms, the past merely exists and is passive. The student's future is what she has the freedom and responsibility to influence, facilitated by effective instruction, "Man shall attain existence only when he is what he projects himself to be" (p.23). The teacher, if viewing the student in existentialist terms, also views each student as an individual—a blank slate, full of potential. The teacher also has the opportunity in existentialism to examine herself and her essence as a teacher.

Sartre believed that "philosophy should endeavour to change people's lives for the better" (Linsenbard, 2010, p. 2). It is for this reason that I draw upon Sartre's ideas as a philosophical foundation and framework to inform this study. Sartre's views on the ability one has to determine one's outcome, his views on an essence that is projected by the self, as well as his very clear view of being and the self as free, make his principles an appropriate choice for this research study.

As a theoretical framework, "existentialism is fundamentally an educational philosophy because it is the theory of human *becoming*" (Feldman, 2009). The teacher and student have the ability to become what they desire to be. In this relationship, the teacher's role is crucial in leading the student to consider and to discover what she can become. Sartre's view of existentialism puts the individual in charge and makes her responsible for what she is and will become. Sartre (2001) writes:

> We mean that man first exists: he materializes in the world, encounters himself, and only afterward defines himself. If man as existentialists conceive of him cannot be defined, it is because to begin with he is nothing. He will not be anything until later, and then he will be what he makes of himself. (p.22)

When existentialism becomes the framework for research in education, it leads to other questions that have framed my research. What does it mean to teach and what does it mean to facilitate? These are not the same. Anyone can teach, but the act or art of facilitating is quite different, particularly in the field of vocal instruction. Many can teach voice by offering sequential exercises, imitation, imagery, ways to release tension, and instruction of aspects of vocal anatomy, but the question remains as to whether or not a compartmentalized approach leads to consistency, emotion, and freedom in singing. Harper (1955) notes, "Existentialism is concerned about the unfolding of the individual as a whole in the situation in which he finds himself" (p. 223). This description parallels much of the task of the vocal instructor. A voice instructor has the opportunity to guide or facilitate the student through this unfolding or self-discovery in voice study. In this approach, the instructor faces her freedom and responsibility in the role of facilitator in the voice studio, while leading the student to explore her freedom and to become more self-aware as a singer and performer. In existentialism, "man is called to know himself; it is not optional and a matter of luxury" (p. 228). These principles give the teacher the opportunity to explore the question of what it means to facilitate as opposed to what it means to teach.

Existentialism has been considered a valuable framework for educational research because of the focus on the individual (Webster, 2002). Webster states that it "allows the framework to be applicable for addressing specific educational issues involving the learner, such as pedagogy" (p. 5). The individual in existentialism has free will and the ability to decide her essence. The teacher who is able and willing to find her essence as an instructor is one who will strive to obtain a varied set of teaching tools upon which she can draw, and one that is willing to face her freedom and responsibility as a facilitator in the voice studio and to use these skills in a flexible manner. Part of the process is for her to understand herself as a teacher, for in understanding herself, she can create her essence as a voice instructor. If the instructor makes the choice to understand herself in existentialist terms, to explore her consciousness, she has an opportunity to engage in self-evaluation. In an existentialist mindset of instruction, one can choose to become the type of instructor who can facilitate consistency and emotional engagement in singing. An existential framework considers the individual "free to choose, holistic, a meaning-maker, able to create self-identity and has authenticity to some degree" (p. 5). In existentialism, the teacher is able to create her own identity as a teacher. An existentialist framework provides teachers with the opportunity to choose, to find their essence as teachers, and to engage in a facilitative relationship in which both the student and teacher explore their freedom in the voice studio. The teacher who is in possession of knowledge of various approaches to vocal instruction has the opportunity, when using an existentialist foundation, to explore the student's individual needs and to facilitate the path for the student to find her essence as a singer. In so doing, the teacher has the opportunity to explore her essence as a teacher. In facing freedom, the teacher is free to choose various approaches, or any combination of them, to help the student find consistency and to engage emotionally in her performances.

To explore these principles further, I present an overview of several of Sartre's existentialist principles: existence (being present in the world as a blank slate full of potential); essence (one's nature, that is created by the person and experience of one's essence); freedom (the ability to make choice about one's course of action, autonomy); choice (the decision one makes by exercising freedom, free will); and responsibility, and the anguish and abandonment that can at times accompany it (Sartre, 2001). The existentialist tenets that will be introduced relate to and are determined by each other.

Existentialist Principles of Jean-Paul Sartre

I begin with the idea of existence. Sartre's existentialism starts from the premise of existence. A human is "a being who exists before he can be defined by any concept of it" (Sartre, 2007, p. 22). The essence of a human comes only after she exists and through the choices that are made; in other words, the image of the self that she projects. In order to understand Sartre's idea of existentialism, it is necessary to understand his ideas about existence and essence. According to this description, "To say that something *exists* is to say that *it is*. To state something's *essence* is to state *what* or *how* it is" (Sartre, 2001, p. 21). Existence and essence are distinct from one another. Sartre (1984) describes existence as our past, present, and future. Each student has a history; however, the existentialist teacher may view a new student as a blank slate, an existing presence with endless potential. Our past exists; however, it is a passive place that we can do nothing about. The present is our time of freedom, consciousness, and choice, and our future is full of possibilities. The teacher must now help the student realize free will and responsibility. The teacher regards the student as being free, and cannot force her ideas or opinions on the student, try to define the student in her own terms, or instruct her to be like the teacher; this would be considered molding a student. Molding or controlling a student is a form of imitation. Instead, the teacher facilitates the student in becoming aware of the best choices, through the teacher's guidance. The student comes to her own conclusions and discoveries. In existentialism, the student exists; however, the essence of the student is what must be discovered and created by the student, albeit guided by an effective teacher. Sartre (2007) explains and clarifies his ideas of existence and essence further. He feels that there is no predetermined human essence and no human nature prior to a human existing: "When we are born, we have no essence as human beings. Only the totality of choices we make in life makes us the people who we are. In this sense we are profoundly free" (Sartre, 2001, p. 25). The voice student comes to study without essence; she merely exists, although she has vocal history. The teacher views the student as someone who is full of potential. There is no predetermined nature for the voice student. Each student will arrive at a higher education music program with various levels of ability and background. Using an existentialist approach, voice teachers can view each student as an individual and one capable of determining her essence as a singer. The sound of a student's voice and her potential cannot be defined by the teacher; it must be discovered by the student through facilitation. The voice teacher is also an individual, free to choose and project her essence as a facilitator of vocal study. In order to understand the ideas of essence and how it can be determined by the individual (in this case, the teacher), one must explore Sartre's ideas centered in being. The idea of being in Sartrean terms is defined as two manners.

Sartre (1984) felt there were two manners of being: *being-for-itself* and *being-in-itself*. Being-for-itself involves our consciousness and our awareness of it. Consciousness and awareness are important and very relevant in vocal instruction and singing. The teacher must be aware and conscious of whether or not the information facilitated to the student is understood. The voice instructor is the guide for the student, helping her make connections and discoveries. A keen awareness and sensitivity to the student through consciousness and awareness is essential in effective vocal instruction. This awareness, focus, and consciousness are necessary in order for a student to gain consistency in singing. The voice teacher should strive to be aware and conscious of the student and should be able to gauge whether or not the student is internalizing and understanding the information given. Some teachers in the voice studio may not be focused on whether or not this information is being translated successfully and are perhaps just focused on accomplishing a certain number of exercises or singing a certain number of songs within in a given lesson. They are thus not as "tuned in" or aware of what the student is experiencing. Perhaps some teachers instruct on "auto-pilot" if they have been teaching for a long time, and perhaps they are not as enthusiastic instructors as at the start of their careers. Being-for-itself, or consciousness and awareness, are also important ideas in the act of singing. A singer or student must be aware—physically aware and conscious of what is going on— while she is singing. If a student is neither focused nor aware, she will likely continue to make the same mistakes (singing with tension, lack of resonance, or poor breath support, for example), furthering inconsistency in singing. For a singer, the body is the instrument; being-for-itself and the elements of consciousness and awareness align with this idea. Everything one does while singing affects the tone, breath, and vocal projection. A singer must multi-task during performance. While singing, the singer must have heightened consciousness and awareness. She must be able to assess and be fully conscious and aware of what is going on with her posture, breath, diction, resonant singing tone, and any potential building of tension in the body, as it will affect her tone, and must be able to address any issues that occur during performance. For example, a singer who has tense shoulders, stiff hands, a tense jaw or tongue, or even locked knees will have a vocal tone that also is tense (Doscher, 1994). Singers are the instrument; the singer must at all times be fully conscious and aware of what she is experiencing while singing, and at the same time be aware and conscious of the musical and emotional elements in a song or aria. A student who is neither aware nor conscious may not be able to be in the moment or emotionally engaged while singing. An observer will generally be able to sense whether the student is engaged or not, as the observer's aesthetic reaction to the singer will reflect her engagement.

Being-in-itself involves how the world external to our consciousness exists. This idea is not as relevant for this study centered on vocal instruction. The world external to consciousness (being-in-itself), as it relates to singing and vocal instruction, is about the singer and teacher being physically present outside of each one's consciousness. This manner of being is not conducive to effective teaching or to gaining consistency and emotional engagement in singing. The ideas of consistency and emotionality and the attempt to instill these in a student require the focus of the teacher to be on the student-teacher relationship, as well as her consciousness and awareness of the individual student. A teacher, for example, who views her existence in the voice studio as being-in-itself will not be completely focused on the collaborative student-teacher relationship within the studio and thus will not be addressing the individual needs of the student, or whether her own facilitation is effective or not. Perhaps her focus is elsewhere, having nothing to do with the student. If the focus of the teacher is on the external world (being-in-itself), beyond the student-teacher relationship without consciousness or awareness of the individual needs of the student, the facilitative relationship with the student may not be effective.

Using the idea of being-for-itself, the teacher is focused on awareness and conscious within herself and within her student. She is conscious and aware of what information the student needs to sing well and consistently, and whether or not she is translating the information to the student effectively. She is also conscious and aware of the student's reaction to her facilitation. She is there for the student as a facilitator. If one views a student in terms relating to being-in-itself, the reaction that the world external to consciousness has to one's singing is not in one's control. In existentialist terms, the idea of being-for-itself has to do with the exploration of consciousness, freedom, and an ability to determine one's outcome. Thus, the idea of being-for-itself appears more relevant than being-in-itself in working towards a student-teacher relationship that might help improve consistency and emotional engagement in students.

Within the idea of being-for-itself there are three components: *facticity, transcendence, and temporality*. Facticity and transcendence are the components of being-for-itself that relate most to the singer as a student and performer. These two terms are dependent on each other. The exploration of one's freedom can lead to transcendence, which can alter facticity. They occur in a state where freedom of choice is exercised. Facticity has several components. First, there are the facts of a person, such as her birth or what she does as a career. Transcendence is related to facticity in that it occurs when one exercises free will and explores freedom. It is the sum of choices, possibilities, and expectations. According to Sartre (1984), "facticity of my place is revealed to me only in and through the free choice which I make of my end" (p. 634). This leads to the concept of freedom and free will.

For Sartre, those exercising freedom can alter facticity through transcendence (the occurrence that comes from exploration of freedom). The voice teacher can explore her freedom to become, project, or transcend, in order to become the type of instructor she wishes to be; the type of instructor who can facilitate consistency and emotional engagement in her students, and thus alter her facticity. A student guided by a voice instructor to explore freedom can alter her facticity as a student. The student, when guided towards her freedom through effective facilitation, can perhaps transcend to find a new facticity, to define or re-define the type of student or singer she is, to influence her essence, and to explore the possibilities of what she can become. Thus, the relation of facticity and transcendence informs the very notion of one's essence.

Let me turn to essence, accordingly. An individual or teacher in being-for-itself (one that is conscious and aware) engaged in the exploration of freedom as teacher and/or student leading to transcendence can alter her facticity and determine her essence. She can become the type of instructor she desires to be. She can be the type of instructor who facilitates and guides consistent and emotional engagement in her voice students.

The idea of essence through choices stems from one's existence. The teacher can help guide the student. The teacher can help make the student aware that she has the ability, and is free, to make the decision to be a willing and open-minded student. The student has made a choice to study at the university level and, consequently, has the ability to choose to obtain as much knowledge and guidance as possible during her years of study. The student has the freedom to take a path or to not take that path; the decision is completely up to the student. Sartre says (2007), "He will not be anything until later, and then he will be what he makes of himself" (p. 22). The student has freedom and free will to determine what she will make of herself as a singer.

One may see, then, how the application of existentialism may help inform the way in which vocal instruction is approached in higher educational institutions. A voice teacher in higher education takes on responsibility and must be ready to accept this reality. The teacher is responsible for both the student and the experience the student has in studying voice at the higher education level. The teacher must help the student to make a connection to the information that he or she wants to student to obtain. The teacher must also instill a sense of responsibility in the student and make the student aware of her part in learning new information, since "man is responsible for what he is" (Sartre, 2007, p. 23). Sartre's message is that there are simply "no excuses" (p. 29). This principle serves to instill the idea of responsibility in both student and teacher. The teacher is responsible for instruction and for helping the student to make a connection. The student is to take an active role in the learning process and is to be a stakeholder in what she will become, without excuses.

When one is in possession of oneself, this creates freedom. Freedom for this study, as discussed in Chapter One, is considered in terms of: artistic freedom, free will, and freedom for the instructor in the facilitative relationship in the voice study to explore various teaching approaches, physically free singing (without tension, and restriction), freedom to determine essence, and artistic freedom in expression. In other words, when the singer is in control, aware of her ability to choose the outcome and result of her actions, she can determine and influence her outcome. Sartre's freedom is one that depends "entirely on the freedom of others" (p. 48). The teacher is faced with her own freedom, as well as the student's. The teacher realizes the choices she makes in instruction will affect the student. Sartre states, "I cannot set my own freedom as a goal without also setting the freedom of others as a goal" (p. 49). The student-teacher relationship viewed through an existentialist lens is one in which both teacher and students explore freedom of choice. The teacher, in this type of relationship, is aware of his or her choice in how to instruct.

According to Sartre's view of existentialism, upon the realization of this freedom and responsibility, one may at times experience both abandonment and anguish. These terms are connected. When one realizes one's freedom, one knows one cannot escape this responsibility, and thus anguish or the emotional burden of the choices one makes may ensue. Sartre believes that humans experience various states of anguish and abandonment (2007). The term abandonment is the realization that we are ultimately alone in our choices. We are free and fully responsible and therefore alone, since "man is free, man is freedom" (p. 29). Man bears the full responsibility for himself, alone. Sartre explains further, "It is we, ourselves, who decide who we are to be" (p. 34). One is abandoned, "in the sense that I find myself suddenly alone and without help engaged in a world for which I bear the whole responsibility" (Sartre, 1984, p. 710). The teacher may encounter the feeling of being abandoned and alone and experience anguish in the realization of her responsibility in instructing a student. According to Sartre (2007), "When we say that man chooses himself, not only do we mean that each of us must choose himself, but also that in choosing himself, he is choosing for all men" (p. 24). A teacher who considers using existentialist principles in her teaching approach may feel her choices and decisions might affect many in a teaching context: the students, the faculty, the institution, and the future pupils of her student. As well, the student may come to the realization that she is ultimately alone and abandoned in determining her own essence. There is a profound responsibility in making choices. The student may become aware that when she is on the stage performing, she is alone and abandoned and solely responsible for her outcome as a student and as a performer. The teacher in this relationship must think of the future of the student when the student is no longer at the institution or when the student must give solo performances, and the teacher must facilitate an ability to make choices, accept responsibility, and face feelings of anguish and abandonment. Sartre (2007) speaks of anguish as "anguish pure and simple, of the kind experienced by all who have borne responsibilities" (p. 27).

Sartre's views on abandonment and anguish perhaps at first glance may appear negative. It is important, however, to note that not all teachers or students may experience a feeling of abandonment or anguish. A teacher considering using existentialist thought may gain the ability to anticipate that the student might feel alone and experience anguish while performing and practicing. Teachers can help the student realize that existentialist ideas such as responsibility and independence in learning can be positive. The teacher is not to mold the student, as this would not respect the freedom of the student or instill responsibility or independence in singing and is therefore ineffective instruction. This inability to sing independently may actually cause feelings of abandonment and anguish for the student, as she may feel that she does not know what she is doing. I have witnessed this look of fear in the eyes—an image of a "deer in the headlights" comes to mind— in many young singers performing on stage. This is a student who is experiencing anguish and feeling abandoned and alone on stage. This is typically noted when a singer is not confident, lacks consistency in singing, and is terrified. One can experience this feeling, also known as "nerves," while on stage. There are different types of nerves. The nerves or anguish of feeling alone and abandoned on stage are the experience of a student who feels ill-prepared or unable to sing independently. This is quite different from a feeling of nervous excitement before stepping out on stage.

Voice instructors strive for their students not to need them at a certain point. Arguably, a key aims for voice instructors to see their students being able to step out on stage alone, fully responsible for their performances, filled with artistic freedom and choice, and able to face any potential feeling of anguish and abandonment. A teacher who molds students is one who teaches through imitation, striving for her students to become copies of the teacher. I content that this will not help a student gain autonomy or independence in singing, nor will it facilitate ways to deal with potential feelings of abandonment and anguish. A voice student must have a consistent manner or technique of singing in order to feel independent, autonomous, free, and responsible as a singer. As well, this consistency can give the student the ability to deal with whatever possible feelings of anguish and abandonment may occur alone in a practice room or while alone on stage performing. In some voice studios, the students sound the same as the teacher, although the teacher may have an entirely different voice type (vocal maturity, range, vocal weight, and color). The teacher who guides or facilitates the student is one who offers information and presents opportunities for the student to come to her own discoveries, and in so doing, facilitates an ability to gain responsibility and independence. Voice instructors should attempt to prepare students and to facilitate the most consistent singing possible for the student. In some cases, however, it is important to note that a student may still experience feelings of anguish and abandonment, even if the teacher has facilitated consistent singing. Some students will experience immense fear, no matter how well their teachers try to prepare them for these feeling of anguish and abandonment.

The teacher, like the student, may also experience feelings of anguish and abandonment with the realization of her immense responsibility as a voice instructor. This can also appear negative at first glance, as noted at the beginning of this discussion regarding the potentially negative view of Sartre's idea of anguish and abandonment. The teacher is responsible for helping the student find consistency in singing and must guide the student to find artistry in singing; this is a great deal of responsibility. A voice instructor can, however, consider an existentialist framework as a way to look at this responsibility in a positive light, and so perhaps can find ways to not feel anguish or abandonment. For example, a teacher using existentialist thought may consider ways to not feel trapped in using just one teaching approach in vocal instruction. Perhaps existentialist thought can free the teacher from a feeling of constraint by offering her the opportunity to explore her freedom to try different teaching approaches. I believe it can be empowering for a teacher to become aware that she can determine her essence as a teacher. She can experience being-for-itself in a way that transcendence happens (the sum of freedom, choices, and possibilities) and have the power to alter her facticity as a voice instructor. As well, a student can be guided to embrace the idea of responsibility in existentialist terms. A student who can be guided to a sense of responsibility and exploration of freedom may have the potential to feel empowered and filled with confidence in performance rather than alone and abandoned. A teacher who uses existentialist principles and encompasses a varied approach may help the student gain consistency in singing. A student who can sing consistently is one that is empowered and confident. A student who feels she has a strong grasp of how to sing consistently may have the ability to step out alone on stage and feel confident and excited to explore the possibilities of what she can experience on stage. In this moment, the student can experience transcendence and, potentially, can give a truly artistic performance. I suggest that existentialist principles can be considered a very positive influence on a teaching approach in vocal instruction.

The next section will explore and further develop the reasons and rationale for choosing to view the student-teacher relationship in the voice studio through an existentialist lens. I will illustrate how existentialism has already influenced a framework for the student-teacher relationship in general education and will continue to argue how existentialist tenets may be considered in a pedagogical approach to vocal instruction. This study represents a way for vocal instructors to consider and reframe how they view vocal instruction in higher education. I suggest that the student-teacher relationship in the higher education voice studio, if viewed through an existentialist lens, can be one that is a collaborative relationship, where both teacher and student can experience growth as artists. In existentialist terms, both teacher and student engage in a relationship based in exploring freedom and responsibility, simultaneously. The voice instructor grows from the experience of instructing the student, just as the student grows and develops in her singing practice. In a relationship that is student-centered, such as one that will be considered in an existentialist framework for this study, a student may acquire an ability to participate in selecting repertoire. This is a part of accepting responsibility and gaining independence. It is also possible, if a student is guided to sing consistently by an effective instructor, for the student and teacher to discuss and analyze the student's individual interpretation of a piece of music, her choices, and her vision for the song. Once a student can sing with vocal consistency, many possibilities of emotional interpretation open, as the student is not distracted and delayed in this process by her lack of consistent singing. I consider that the student-teacher relationship based in existentialist thought can be one that is considered collaborative, in the sense that it is student-centered and the path that the course of study takes depends very much on the student and her progress. There can be an extended discussion between teacher and student on vocal development. It is the duty and responsibility of voice instructors to help students find a consistent vocal technique and to make an emotional connection to the music they are studying. Once an instructor accepts a student into her private studio, she is taking on the responsibility of this student. An existentialist overview of instruction can perhaps act as a guideline for a novice, or even experienced, teacher. At the same time, perhaps it will give the teacher the opportunity to explore her own freedom and potential as an instructor, while leading the student to consistent singing and emotionally.

Van Manen (1991), when discussing the tact and art of teaching, suggests that novice teachers must spend time finding out who they are. Perhaps existentialism can offer both novice voice teachers in higher education and currently practicing teachers the opportunity to reflect on who they are as instructors. I suggest that existentialism offers a unique way to view oneself as a voice teacher. It can present voice teachers with ways to reflect on responsibility, ways to think about guiding students to sing consistently and with emotion, and opportunities to think about what it means to face freedom and free will as these can be explored in the student-teacher relationship in the voice studio. It can present the opportunity to examine effectiveness as a facilitator of vocal development. For voice teachers, the goal should be to help the student gain independence, to not need the instructor and to, eventually, no longer hold status as a student but rather as an artist. A teacher must find effective ways to ensure this transition happens for a voice student. The teacher must find a way to guide the student in voice study without being overbearing or interfering with the student's freedom and free will. She must act as a role model and facilitator, and take on the responsibility of instructing each student while finding a way to maintain a balance in which the student is guided but not molded or controlled in her vocal development or interpretive choices.

The pedagogical methods that were examined in the previous chapter do not sufficiently address the student-teacher relationship in the voice studio. They focus on instructing certain aspects of vocal technique, but do not address the complete student and his or her experience in vocal study. In considering existentialism as a framework for a pedagogical approach to vocal instruction, it may be possible to examine the effectiveness of the student-teacher relationship and perhaps to offer a way of viewing the entire student. This approach attempts to instruct the student in a method that can encompass all aspects of instructing vocal technique and bringing the student to the level where she can explore artistic freedom and interpretation of music. It is a challenge for a student to reach this level of freedom if she is constantly distracted by the inability to sing consistently.

The next section will explore existentialism and how it has already been used as a theoretical framework for education. I will discuss the principles of responsibility and freedom in further detail and argue further how they can be considered in vocal instruction.

EXISTENTIALISM, EDUCATION, AND EFFECTIVE VOCAL INSTRUCTION

This section provides the underpinning foundation of how existentialism has been applied to education theory in terms of the student-teacher relationship, humanistic education, and the individual and her experience and potential. I start with existentialism and its application to education to establish an *a priori* assumption that the principles of existentialism have relevance for educational theory and practice. In drawing upon this literature, I then extend this discussion to consider how an existentialist framework may inform the way in which educators consider the art of vocal instruction in higher education to mitigate inconsistent and unemotional singing in students.

I begin with some examples of how existentialist principles have been considered as a theoretical framework in general education and illustrate how they might be also be viewed as a framework for vocal instruction. I then discuss central ideas in Sartre's existential principles: responsibility and freedom, and how these may be considered beneficial in the student-teacher relationship in the voice studio. I will argue that these principles can provide consideration of a student-teacher relationship in the voice studio that strives to inspire individuality and responsibility, and thus leads students to gain independence and autonomy in singing and an ability to find freedom in artistic expression.

The principles of responsibility and freedom are interrelated in existentialist thought, which may have relevance in the application to vocal instruction. This will be discussed further in the following section. The concept of responsibility will be explored in existentialist terms for vocal instruction. The voice instructor is responsible for the student in this facilitative relationship and should make every effort to help the student reach a level of consistency in singing. Vocal instructors are called upon to facilitate consistent singing in their students. In order to be effective, this requires an ability to facilitate consistency. In this study, this ability will be considered by viewing an existentialist framework including the flexibility that allows for using varying pedagogical approaches. In this vein, the student can also be encouraged to take on responsibility in the learning process. She can be made aware that her outcome will be the sum of the elements put into the process by the student. In taking on this responsibility, both teacher and student face and explore their freedom in the student-teacher relationship.

The principle of freedom will be explored later in this section in terms of free will, choice, physically free singing, and artistic freedom. When considering the notion of freedom in an existentialist framework, an instructor is in a position to present the student with the ability to choose, to have a stake in what she will project and what she will become as a singer. The notion of freedom for the voice instructor will be viewed in part as the opportunity to choose and to explore freedom in this student-teacher relationship. In existentialist terms, she may have the chance to project the type of voice instructor she wishes to be or become, and to alter her facticity (the sum of the facts about the individual) to become the type of instructor who can facilitate consistency and emotional engagement in her students. Consideration of an existentialist outlook on instruction may also offer choice. A voice instructor may wish to consider acting upon free will to choose how she will instruct her students, whether or not she will be an effective facilitator of voice, and how she will accomplish this—and then make strides to do so.

The Application of Existentialism to General Education

The parallels of existentialism, education, and the student-teacher relationship are notable. In order to understand the application of existentialist principles as part of education theory, it is important to examine the historical perspective of their application to general education prior to discussing the principles of responsibility and freedom in more detail and how these may also be considered in vocal instruction in higher education today.

Existentialist ideas and the possibilities of an education based in existentialism were explored in the preliminary stages of the existentialists' prominence by Van Cleve Morris (1954). His research explored the student-teacher relationship and how the teacher, using an existentialist approach, could strive towards educating the individual learner. Morris' (1961) early research centred on pedagogy for children based in existentialism and the opinion that education should provide a private and individual experience for the child. Morris examined the possibilities of existentialism in education at a time when not many researchers had considered the application of existentialist thought to education. He considered how existentialism could be a fitting foundation for an educational teaching method. Morris writes that existentialist teachers "will be more interested in developing the affective side of man, his capacity to love, to appreciate, to respond emotionally to the world around him" (p. 255).

The idea of responding "emotionally" and perhaps developing a pedagogical approach to elicit capacity for an emotional response and experience draws parallels to voice students and instructors searching for ways to emotionally engage and find appreciation in music. Existentialist principles may offer ways for instructors to aid in the development of an emotional reaction to music from voice students. Morris explains that the content of what the individual puts in this private experience is quite important, indicating "the existentialist educator is necessarily interested in having the youngster fill his quiet moments with the personal judgements he must make concerning his own life" (Morris, 1961, p. 59). In this way, the personal judgements to which an individual becomes attentive bridge her awareness of freedom and responsibility in learning. One can also look at how progress might be made in voice study when the student is reminded by the instructor that her outcome will be in her own control. This idea and "quiet moments" and "personal judgements" parallel many of the experiences of a vocal student. The daily rituals of a vocal student require that she be in a state of being with a quiet reflective mind that offers the opportunity for the student to explore freedom (artistic) and free will in interpretation of music and text, such as can occur in a practice room for a singer.

In addition to the awareness of self, Morris discusses the idea of responsibility, giving the student a stake in her learning through choice, where "the existentialist educator would seem to be committed to the task of developing the choice-making power in the individual" (Morris, 1961, p. 256). In this way, the emphasis becomes on fostering the individual's capacity to both be attentive in quiet contemplation and, further, to understand the judgements and decisions that are required within the self. In understanding the discretionary choices that are involved, the voice student becomes empowered, and a stakeholder in her own vocal development.

Education theory based in existentialist thought emphasises the focus placed on the individual student holistically. It looks for ways to instruct the entire student and not just certain aspects of the individual. In some respects, existentialism and its application to education gained prominence as perhaps a criticism of or response to previous teaching approaches such as a mass-produced or rote method of teaching. Harper (1955) states, "The existentialist does want to educate the total man, not just one or another side of him" (p. 223). This statement critiques the idea of the mass-produced, rote process of instruction. What existentialism offers is a way to consider how the relationship between the student and teacher requires that instructors develop a perspective that develops the students' individualised needs and an understanding of the role of responsibility and freedom in the learning process and student-teacher relationship.

Other reactions against previously considered education theories encouraged some to promote existentialism as a beneficial theoretical framework for education. Carole Lieberman (1985) reviewed several approaches, such as *essentialist* and *behaviourist* approaches to teaching, and considered approaches based in existentialism more effective. The essentialist considers ideas based in fostering innate qualities, while the behaviourist views the student as a passive receiver of cultural and historic information. A behaviourist approach also considers that specific cultural influences are to be placed on a child. An essentialist student-teacher relationship is teacher-centered. It is an approach whereby students learn of their culture through a core curriculum. A behaviourist student-teacher relationship has at its center the goal of a change in student behavior through conditioning and response. The existentialist student-teacher relationship prioritizes the instructor as a guide, and the central focus resides on the student.

A voice instructor who considers the student in existentialist terms repositions the roles of the student and the teacher (Lieberman, 1985). Although the teacher is responsible for guiding the student to make connections, the focus still remains on the student and how to facilitate the information to the student in the most effective and individualised way. In an existentialist approach, there is no behavior to change in a student as is evident in the behaviorist approach. Many of the behaviourist approaches represent a student-teacher relationship in which the student is treated as an object, not a subject or an individual capable of an experience. The instructor considering the influence of existentialist principles may feel that a mass approach to education is not a good pedagogical approach (Lieberman, 1985). This has parallels to the teaching practices that may be used in some voice studios, where a teacher has each of her students sing the same rote exercises without addressing the specific needs of each student. This may occur in the scientific, and in some contemporary, approaches to teaching that were discussed in the previous section. A scripted lesson will likely not inspire individual learning or interpretation and may present a challenge for a student to develop consistent singing. Lieberman states, "Existentialists do not want, by advocating equal opportunities for all, mass education, employing assembly line techniques. Mass education is similar to rote learning in vocal instruction. In this approach, the student repeats what she has been taught in the classroom" (p. 325). A student educated in a mass setting is not treated as an individual. A voice student instructed with the same exercises that everyone else sings is also not treated as an individual. Each singer has specific needs to address to find consistency in singing, and this simply cannot be accomplished by singing scripted exercises. Yet the features criticised in mass education can commonly be found in the practices of vocal instruction. It is not uncommon for voice students to repeat a set of rote exercises without a point of reference. In emphasizing this task, the repetition underemphasises the importance of the singer finding her individuality. Arguably, the rote learning does little to foster consistency in singing or artistic freedom. In order for a student to find her individual sound and consistency in singing, the voice instructor has the responsibility to guide the student as an individual, with specific student-focused or individualised instruction. Lieberman states, "The teacher must guard against fostering his/her own values upon students and must inculcate a feeling of self-reliance in each of them" (p. 324). This view speaks of the idea of instilling responsibility in the student. A voice student who is instructed to be self-reliant is a singer who will find consistency in singing.

In existentialist terms, the student merely exists full of potential. The responsibility and goal of the instructor can be an attempt to find and guide the discovery of the essence of each voice student, starting from the beginning, through effective instruction geared towards each individual. An existentialist environment in a voice studio may inform the student-teacher relationship in ways that encourage consistency in singing, including personal autonomy, independence, and artistic choices or artistic freedom of expressions. This idea may not be present in a studio in which a student is not led towards her individual freedom, such as one using an approach based solely in science, for example. A teaching approach based in science and anatomy appears rigid and without flexibility, and it may not instill consistency in singing or inspire creativity in the student. As well, a student instructed through imagery may not develop a feeling of self-reliance, independence, or autonomy in singing.

Others have explored existentialism as a positive philosophical foundation in education. Using an existentialist approach as a framework, the teacher creates an environment in which the student comes to her own understanding. Martin and Loomis (2007) contend, "No single set of learning outcomes is appropriate for all students" (p. 52). Each student has different needs and must be approached individually to elicit appropriate outcomes. A voice student will have a different set of learning outcomes from each of her classmates. This idea is unlike differentiated instruction, which considers attentiveness to learning. An existentialist framework goes further and considers the notion of fostering responsibility and freedom in vocal instruction, attempting to offer a way for the voice instructor to address the learner (the singer) and to find individual outcomes specific for each student aiding in fostering artistry in singing. Each voice student will develop a different essence as a singer, bringing with her a different tone and emotional experience; therefore, drawing upon existentialist thought and addressing the student as an individual may offer a way to help the student find her essence as a singer. In understanding the role of the teacher and student in existentialism, it is important to understand how responsibility and freedom inform this relationship, and how this may have particular relevance for vocal instructors in higher education. The next section discusses each tenet in detail and considers their application to vocal instruction and the student-teacher relationship.

Responsibility and Freedom in the Student-Teacher Relationship

Responsibility and freedom are interconnected in existentialist thought. One cannot exist without the other. In order to find and explore freedom, one must face responsibility. Certain distinguishing aspects of responsibility and freedom are important in their application to vocal instruction. The notion of responsibility is viewed differently from the perspective of the student and that of the instructor; each individual has a different role in responsibility in the voice studio. As well, the notion of freedom translates to something different for the student and the instructor. Briefly, freedom from the instructor's perspective is her creation of her essence as instructor. For the student, freedom is also the notion of creating essence, but as well it is exploring freedom in artistic expression. Let me turn first to the notion of responsibility.

Responsibility

In an existential theoretical approach to vocal instruction and, specifically, to the voice student, responsibility is the precursor to exploring artistic freedom. In order to be able to explore and find artistic freedom, the student must first have responsibility for her instrument and an ability to sing consistently and with technical facility. In order for the student to gain and face this responsibility, and to find consistency, she must be instructed by an effective voice instructor, one who is also responsible and who explores freedom in facing her responsibility as a voice instructor. The student also explores a certain level of freedom of choice while engaging in vocal study that, one hopes, will lead to consistency in singing. The student can explore free will to decide whether or not to take on the responsibility of learning to sing correctly. Thus, these principles are both interconnected and distinct from each other. I begin, accordingly, with responsibility.

In existentialist thought, the individual is charged with being responsible for her outcome and what she will become (Sartre, 1984, 2007). This idea will be explored in relation to both student and instructor in this section. For the student, this notion will be explored in terms of the student taking on an active and engaged role in her learning process, in her vocal development. In existentialist thought, the teachers' awareness of responsibility and her accepting it is crucial.

The notion of responsibility for a student means she is charged with determining her own individual outcome (Sartre, 1984, 2001, 2007). In other words, she is a stakeholder in her education, progress, and its eventual outcome (Bowers, 1965; Dhawan, 2005; Morris, 1954). The student in existentialist thought has the ability to determine and control what she will become. In order to find what she will become, she must take an active role in the process of becoming, hold herself accountable, and face her responsibility in the student-teacher relationship in her own learning environment. When considering this idea in the learning environment in a voice studio in higher education, it is important for the student to be aware of and to have responsibility in learning to gain vocal consistency. The student must consider the information being facilitated by her voice instructor and take an engaged role in imprinting the correct way to sing. This requires awareness, commitment, and focus on the part of the student. In this realisation of responsibility, the student becomes aware that the decisions she makes in her course of voice study will determine the type of singer and performer she will become. A student who does not realise or embrace her responsibility may just mindlessly sing exercises in a practice room without focus, learning vocal repertoire on a superficial level. She may never attain consistency in singing or develop the ability to explore artistry. The singer who is not responsible for her own instrument and does not take an active role in the student-teacher relationship will likely continue singing inconsistently. She may not experience a great deal of vocal development.

Awareness of responsibility by the student and acting upon it are necessary in order for her to be able to learn to sing independently and with autonomy. The terms independence and autonomy are related. I believe that consistency in singing is the sum of independence and autonomy and is gained through a student's awareness of responsibility. The ability to sing independently is the ability to sing with consistency in a practice room, in a lesson, and in performance with confidence and with no doubt as to how to use one's instrument properly. The independent singer can step out on the stage fully aware of her voice; she has autonomy and complete ownership of her instrument. Autonomy, for a singer, is an ability to be in control of her voice technically and to make decisions in performance. These can be decisions such as how to control and manipulate the voice while singing, how to alter one's resonant singing tone, or how much breath one uses. These autonomic choices are not to be confused with the artistic choices that will be discussed further in the next section.

Consistency can also be considered technical proficiency and facility in singing. With vocal consistency, independence, ownership, or technical proficiency, the singer can make autonomous decisions leading to exploring artistic interpretation. The relationship of responsibility and freedom are connected, they are dependent upon each other. A student cannot experience artistry without taking responsibility for gaining independence and autonomy (consistency) in singing. This awareness of responsibility and the guidance towards consistency that leads the artistry in singing must come from an effective instructor. The next paragraphs explore the role of the teacher in responsibility. In the following paragraphs, I will show how although the role of the student is important in facing responsibility and taking an active role in the learning process, this cannot be accomplished without an effective instructor. The role of the instructor in the student-teacher relationship in the voice studio is crucial. The voice instructor is the guide facing the responsibility of helping the student make connections and find artistry in singing.

A reciprocal relationship occurs in the teacher's awareness of her responsibility in the student-teacher relationship. The teacher is the guide helping the individual or student, in this case, become aware of responsibility, guiding her towards freedom. The instructor's view of the individual, in light of Sartre's views, and her ability to project her outcome may be considered influential in a student-teacher relationship. Burstow (1983) notes:

> Whether the helper be called teacher or therapist, Sartre is asking him to help the human being come to terms with his individual project, accept his freedom and facticity, and emerge as the unique human being that he is. (p. 180)

In this setting, the teacher is the guide. The instructor is there to guide her students to take on responsibility; she is there to help them define their essence and uniqueness, while determining her own outcome as instructor as well. This idea can also be considered in vocal instruction. The instructor acts as the guide for the student to help her face responsibility and find consistency in singing. This guidance comes from an effective voice instructor in a facilitative student-teacher relationship. She is responsible for instructing the student as an individual to find consistency (autonomy and independence) in singing. Patenaude-Yarnell (2003) speaks of guiding the voice student to be responsible: "When a singer is guided into discovering the elements of beautiful singing, rather than always being told how to do it, the results are usually more gratifying" (p. 255). The student who is guided to be responsible for her voice is empowered and more confident. Once independent, she does not need her teacher to make her sing consistently, but rather has the ability to sing well on her own. An effective vocal instructor will strive to bring her students to a level where they no longer need her as a teacher.

A voice instructor who considers an existentialist framework may find she becomes more effective by obtaining an ability to lead her students to independence. She then perhaps can facilitate the type of singing that gives students the opportunity to sing a wider variety of repertoire and the ability to learn music quickly, as they will be able to work more independently. A view of the voice instructor in an existentialist framework may offer ways to consider instilling responsibility through the use of the existentialist notion of no excuses in the student-teacher relationship. This means making the student aware that she is fully responsible for her own outcome. The instructor is the guide; however, the voice student must work hard and be engaged. The instructor may also wish to consider existentialist thought to encourage the student not to be indifferent to the process of vocal study. Sartre (1984) defines indifference as being a form of blindness: "We are dealing with a kind of blindness with respect to others. I do not suffer this blindness as a state. I *am* my own blindness" (p. 495). The instructor, when viewing vocal instruction through an existentialist lens, may be presented with ways to encourage the student to be engaged in learning and not blind, as Sartre speaks of it, in learning, helping her to face her own responsibility.

Considering the notion of responsibility in an existentialist framework for vocal instruction may present the instructor with an awareness of her role in the student-teacher relationship; that is, her responsibility to guide the student in vocal technique, using as many descriptions or pedagogical approaches as necessary to help the student make a connection to consistent singing. As well, the instructor must assist the student not to feel abandoned or in anguish when facing the responsibility of learning to sing consistently, but rather to view this responsibility positively. The student can be made aware by her instructor that facing responsibility can give her the opportunity to project the essence of the singer that she would like to become. In a student-teacher relationship based in existentialism, the instructor may be presented with ways to convince the student that this responsibility is beneficial and may help the student give better performances, as she will be an independent singer. A student guided to accept responsibility gains consistency—meaning independence and autonomy—which leads to an ability to make choices in artistry. These choices can lead to better and more engaged performances. An emotionally engaged singer is a better performer. This concept will be explored in more detail in the discussion of freedom. I believe that a voice instructor who encourages responsibility and who guides her students to be focused and to be stakeholders in finding vocal consistency (independence and autonomy) is an effective vocal instructor, whereas an instructor who cannot guide her students to responsibility or vocal consistency is not an effective instructor and will instead further the prevalence of inconsistent and unengaged singing.

The parallels of the notion of the instructor being responsible for the student and the offer of individualised instruction as found in existential frameworks for education are notable and may also be considered in vocal instruction. The idea of individualised instruction is also found in humanistic education. Humanistic education is influenced by existentialist principles. Humanistic methods of education emphasize the individual, responsibility, flexibility, facilitation, freedom, individual experience, emotions, guiding discoveries, students' worth, and values. The relationship of student and teacher is the most influential and essential part of a learning environment with the teacher as the guide (Rogers & Freiberg, 1994). In the humanistic relationship, the student is considered responsible and free; in other words, the student has responsibility for her outcome, and an ability to make choices in the relationship where the teacher acts as the guide.

An examination of traits in humanistic education considered effective in instruction shows that a teacher who can facilitate should be real and genuine. "When the facilitator is a real person, being what she is, entering into a relationship with the learner without presenting a front or façade, she is much more likely to be effective" (Rogers & Freiberg, 1994, p. 154). These traits are of particular relevance when facilitating for inexperienced, vulnerable voice students. The student-teacher relationship in the voice studio must be real and genuine, without pretense. A voice student is quite vulnerable and sensitive; the student is the instrument, so any indication of a lack of genuine and positive intent on the part of the instructor can negatively affect the student's experience and perhaps development. A voice student places her trust in the instructor. The student should feel that her instructor has her best interests in mind and will try every approach necessary to ensure the student learns how to sing well. Sometimes, a teacher may give up and disengage in lessons. Perhaps this teacher is not facing the responsibility she has taken on. It is also possible that the teacher does not have an effective teaching approach to help the student make a connection to the material that she wishes to translate to the student.

Responsibility and the role of the instructor in voice study may be further considered and examined through discussion of the difference between the notions of teaching voice and facilitating voice. If responsibility is central, then there is a clear awareness of the way in which an instructor must position herself in fostering and facilitating this increasing level of responsibility. Rogers and Freiberg (1994) expressed concern about "teachers" as opposed to "facilitators." A teacher, for example, in the voice studio, may offer students just a set of repetitive, scripted rote exercises without connecting how the exercises can help the student find her resonant tone and other elements of consistent singing. A facilitator is the type of instructor who will ensure that students become aware of their resonant tone and all other aspects of singing, using as many exercises, approaches, or examples as necessary while also discussing breath, posture, tension, an emotional connection to the song, and experiencing the song that is being studied. A teaching approach based in existentialist underpinnings may be considered as a way to facilitate learning vocal technique and foster consistent singing, and as a way for the singer to explore artistry. "I cannot stress too strongly how much I wish that someone could wave that magic wand and change teaching to facilitation" (Rogers and Freiberg, p. 171). A student will have an arduous task trying to find her individual sound and consistency in singing unless facilitated or guided by a knowledgeable instructor who understands her responsibility. As well, an instructor who considers the notions of freedom and free will is willing to give her student responsibility in finding consistency in singing. This freedom and facilitation go far beyond just learning the basic techniques of singing; it also applies to how a singer will eventually interpret a song's text and character when she sings repertoire.

In examining the responsibility of an instructor in facilitating voice in a humanistic environment, one can conclude that a voice instructor offering individualised vocal instruction specific to each students' needs may offer a way to promote more consistency in singing. An individualised, flexible approach may be considered effective in vocal instruction. The student-teacher relationship in the voice studio is a humanistic relationship. It is very much centered on the individual, and her experience, discovery, and emotions. Discovery for a voice student is the discovery of her voice and an awareness of an emotional experience in music. This discovery may happen when a student is instructed as an individual. Bowers (1965) says, "The essence he creates is a product of his choices and will vary from individual to individual" (p. 223). This idea is quite complementary to vocal instruction, the idea of instructing the individual, and the discoveries that can transpire for a student when instructed in this manner.

The student instructed with an individualised focus may discover the possibility of learning to sing consistently, as the focus is on addressing the individual needs of each singer, which may lead to consistency. Many voice instructors may not use an individualised approach. Some may use compartmentalised approaches that appear to not be individualised, such as the scientific, natural, and imagery-based, as well as some contemporary, approaches. A scientific or contemporary approach, as previously discussed, may rely upon scripted exercises; while a natural approach relies on release of tension, and possibly leaves the student without complete vocal development. Teachers using approaches based in imagery may assist the student in a lesson, but this approach is not individualised in that it fails to offer ways for the student to engage in self-discovery or to find consistency in practicing. A student who has no concrete information upon which to rely in a practice room will find it hard to discover her sound and to gain consistency, independence, and autonomy in singing. These approaches do not appear individualised but are instead compartmentalized. These pedagogical approaches appear to address just some aspects of singing. They appear to fail at addressing a complete singer and all aspects of what makes a complete singer and appear to not show effective or responsible instruction. A complete singer is one who is instructed to have consistency in all aspects of singing; not just compartmentalized components such as posture or breath, but all aspects including breath, posture, resonance, lack of tension, and vocal agility. Leading from consistency, the complete singer may then explore musicianship and artistry, and will experience music at a deep emotional level.

It is clear that the student has ownership in responsibility but is not alone in this responsibility; the instructor helps form the student-teacher relationship in the voice studio and her role is crucial. A reciprocal relationship occurs when the instructor becomes aware of her responsibility. The voice instructor in this relationship is the guide and facilitator of consistent singing. As discussed, consistency in singing is the precursor to be able to explore the idea of freedom that will be discussed in the next section. The student must be guided to sing consistently in all aspect of singing in order to gain independence and autonomy. This facilitation must come from an instructor who has responsibility. This type of instructor is one that is effective, and that has an ability to offer individualized and flexible instruction using a number of approaches necessary to help the student reach a level of consistency in singing.

Many teaching approaches such as those mentioned in this section and previous chapters appear ineffective. In the voice studio, these approaches fall short in offering students an ability to reach a high level of vocal consistency, which consequently limits a student's ability to explore freedom in artistry. Consideration of existentialist principles can present voice instructors with ways to view and reconsider responsibility in their relationships. This individualized, flexible pedagogical approach may help facilitate consistency and emotional engagement in singing and be a way for both student and teacher to discover what they can become. Attentiveness to the role of responsibility may provide voice instructors with opportunities to consider how they think about students and about inconsistent and unengaged singing. In considering a humanistic relationship in the voice studio, the student-teacher relationship is one in which the instructor is quite important. A voice instructor viewing a humanistic environment with an existentialist framework may reflect and discover that she wishes to obtain teaching tools to facilitate aspects of vocal instruction in an effective manner. The next section will explore the idea of freedom in the student-teacher relationship in the voice studio, offering ways to consider promoting flexible vocal instruction that will lead to consistency and engagement in singing.

Freedom

The guiding principles of freedom in Sartre's existentialist thought center on free will and choice (Sartre, 1984, 2001, 2007). In considering the broader existentialist principle of freedom for this study, I apply the notion of freedom as well to the choices and judgments one makes in artistry and in physically free singing. I examine the notion of freedom for the voice student first, followed by an examination of freedom for the voice instructor. In considering the notion of freedom for the voice student for this study, I examine several aspects of this principle. My first consideration is the ability to sing physically free. This study also explores free will to define essence. Finally, I consider freedom in artistic choice. This all occurs once the student has gained an ability to sing with consistency. In examining the notion of freedom for the voice instructor in this study, I will consider free will and choice as they may apply to determining the essence of a voice instructor.

For a singer, the body is the instrument; any lack of physical freedom will negatively affect the tone and cause discomfort (Bunch, 1997; Doscher, 1994; & Miller, 1986, 1996, 2004). An inability to sing consistently or freely is disconcerting, and the cause of much stress and feelings of discouragement. However, once the singer has gained consistency and physically free singing, she experiences a sense of freedom, in the sense that she feels released, empowered, and full of possibilities for emotional exploration of music and text. Conversely, the singer who has an ability to sing with consistency is one who has independence and autonomy in singing. Specifically, she has an ability to step out on stage, sing in a practice room, or learn a new piece of music with the self-reliance and confidence that she is using her instrument in a proficient and healthy manner. Once the student has gained this consistency, she has freedom in singing: a physical freedom. This means a relaxed, effortless, released, and free tone. Her body is free and there to act as the instrument, the resonator for the voice without restriction in the tone or tension in the body.

Following the exploration of freedom as the idea of physically free and consistent singing, I also consider the notion of freedom as free will in determining one's essence. When considering the singer and a view of vocal instruction through an existentialist lens, one may wish to consider that the student can determine her essence as a singer and performer. This idea has some parallels to the idea of responsibility, in that the student is a stakeholder. The singer who has been guided to face responsibility with consistency gained in singing, now has further options to determine her essence as a singer. In existentialist thought, a person has the freedom to choose her essence and her outcome and what she will become (Sartre, 2007). This idea may also be considered in a view of voice study and the student. The singer has the ability to determine her essence, the type of singer she will be. In existentialist thought, one's essence is not predetermined. Considering the voice student in existentialist terms, the singer and her voice merely exist, and the exploration of freedom and free will may help the singer determine her essence; that is, the essence of her tone and her emotional experience in music. This is what is to be discovered and created by the singer. The student is free to explore her unique sound and the possibilities of how she can develop it even further once she has gained independence and consistency in singing. This idea may present a view of the possibilities of what the student can become. Bowers (1965) states, "The essence he creates is a product of his choices" (p. 223). This statement refers to free will and choice in existentialist thought. In existentialist thought, the individual determines her essence through free will, through choice, and by deciding her own outcome. She has a say in determining the type of individual she will become. The individual is in control of her outcome, which is the sum of her choices. When considering this idea for the voice student, these choices are not predetermined, as the individual singer decides and creates her essence. The singer has the ability to decide if she will become a consistent singer or not and can be a part of the process of becoming one. As well, once she reaches a level of consistency, the choices she makes in performance and interpretation of music determine the type of artist she will be. These choices in performance are often spontaneous and are therefore individual and not pre-determined. The sum of these choices creates the essence of a singer.

Perhaps the most important examination of freedom when considering the voice student in existentialist terms is the idea of artistic freedom, and the consequent creative possibilities to sing consistently. The independent, autonomous, and technically proficient singer has vast possibilities in her exploration of artistic freedom. The possibilities will vary from student to student, as no voice is the same as another. No emotional experience that a singer brings to a piece of music is the same as another. The voice student may consider an exploration of freedom as a way to consider expressive ideas in performance. For example, she may consider the use of expressive ideas, such as dynamic coloring for emotional effect, tempo variation, facial expression, body language, and expressive use of pronunciation and diction.

A singer who is able to explore her freedom through an individual and expressive interpretation of a piece of vocal music is more engaging to hear and see for an audience member. This idea can be explained further with the comparison between a singer on stage who is technically proficient, but does not explore freedom and lacks emotional engagement, and a singer who is proficient and also explores freedom. In the latter case, the singer tends to be more expressive and thus more engaging to watch perform. There is a great deal of difference in these two singers. Someone who appears to have no focus or emotion in her eyes can be considered a "deer in the headlights" on stage. She may sing with technical facility but is un-engaging and expressionless. A further analogy to illustrate this idea of lack of engagement is suggested by the manner in which one might lecture to a class or present a paper in a conference. A lecturer or speaker may have a great deal of knowledge or facility in the material; however, if she speaks in a low, timid voice without inflection, lacks eye contact with her audience, and appears uncomfortable, this person is not engaging her audience. The audience's reaction to this person may be boredom. A similar reaction may also occur while watching an un-engaging or expressionless singer.

Existentialism presents the teacher with a chance to look at herself as an instructor, to examine free will, and to make the decision to be a stakeholder responsible for helping each voice student uniquely. This concept parallels the idea of free will in relation to the student in that it also involves the idea of responsibility and being a stakeholder in the process. [22] As previously mentioned, some aspects of responsibility and freedom are interconnected and some aspects are distinct. No student is the same, nor does one have the same vocal issues to address as another. The voice instructor may consider the idea of essence as an opportunity to make choices that determine her outcome as a teacher. Morris (1954) remarks, "The way to the good life, or as the existentialist would put it, the authentic life, is for each individual human being to begin realising himself by asserting his individuality and making his own choices" (p. 257). The voice instructor can make choices to determine her essence and perhaps choose if she wishes to be an effective facilitator of vocal technique who may lead her students to find consistency in singing. She may choose to facilitate her students to become independent and autonomous singers who can explore artistic freedom in performance.

In addition to freedom of choice and free will in determining essence, the voice instructor is also presented with freedom of choice in deciding what pedagogical approaches may lead to more consistent singing for her students. As each student is unique, the vocal instructor has available to her any number of approaches that may facilitate consistency and thus guide students towards their artistic freedom. Existentialism and the notions of free will do not prescribe one particular approach, but rather suggest attentiveness to the particular individuals' needs by considering the various options and approaches by an instructor. In this way, the existentialist vocal instructor cannot be complacent in her practices but, rather "encourages individual creativity and imagination more than copying and imitating established models" (Nayak and Rao, 2008, p. 16). Each student's voice is individual and like a fingerprint. It would be beneficial for a voice teacher to have an effective way to approach each student to discover this individuality and facilitate consistency, leading the student to artistic freedom and emotional engagement in singing.

---

[22] The process in this study is the study of vocal technique and development and what is entailed in vocal study: lessons, practice song preparation, translation, learning notes and performance preparation, for example.

An existentialist approach does not advocate a natural (do nothing) approach, or an "anything goes" approach to vocal instruction. Rather, it is a way to consider an effective teacher who is proficient in various approaches of vocal instruction. With this facility, the instructor can explore freedom in the student-teacher relationship to choose to facilitate instruction for her students depending on the specific needs that are presented in lessons. The voice student can present a unique challenge for a voice instructor, as compared to other instrumental instructors. The voice student's body is the instrument, with the potential of having any number of technical issues change in weekly lessons or in student performances. The student is not an inanimate object such as a piano or cello. For example, singers can develop illness or develop postural issues that affect vocal tone. New tensions may arise in the body, affecting breath, throat construction, or an ability to sing with resonance; or other unexpected changes may occur. For example, if a student presents herself in a weekly lesson with a great deal of physical tension, perhaps the instructor can consider exploring freedom in choosing one of the contemporary approaches to facilitate release of tension and more grounded breath in the body. Perhaps the next week, the same student may not be able to access a resonant singing tone and, in this case, the instructor may wish to choose a more scientific approach to illustrate how the voice functions, and to present ways to mitigate this difficulty in finding her resonant singing tone. Perhaps this same individual, once she has reconnected with her resonant singing tone in the lesson cannot emotionally connect to the song she is studying. This may be a time for the instructor to use freedom to choose imagery and imagination to help the student find meaning in the song text, thus helping her make an emotional connection. In an existentialist framework, the exploration of freedom and choice may be effective in facilitating consistency and emotional engagement in students. An existentialist framework requires that instructors draw upon a number of approaches to guide the student through any technical issues presented.

Creating and facilitating an environment in the student-teacher relationship based in freedom is considered beneficial in arts education (Greene, 1973, 1995; & Naples, 1971). Naples (1971) says, "Existentialism urges educators to adopt an attitude of openness and freedom in the classroom that is appropriate to an arts program aimed at developing aesthetic sensitivity" (p. 29). This existentialist view can also be presented for consideration in the higher education voice studio. A voice instructor who is willing to explore her freedom may discover that in using an existentialist framework for instruction she can foster an open and creative environment in the studio, one which may help inspire the student to explore the possibilities of aesthetic sensitivity. This idea of aesthetic sensitivity can be defined in vocal study as an emotional connection, an awareness of and a new sensitivity towards music and text.

In this light, the instructor can be viewed as one who can also present a new and fresh view of music and give this to her students. According to Greene (1973), "The teacher must personally intend to bring about certain changes in students' outlooks; he must mean to enable them to perform in particular ways, to do particular tasks, to impose increasingly complex orders upon their world" (p. 70). The voice instructor considering an existentialist framework is presented with the opportunity to make a commitment to bring about a change in outlook such as Greene (1973) speaks of, in order to help students realise what they can become as singers.

Learning how to sing consistently is arduous, but necessary and a precursor to being able to unlock the free artist within. Greene (1995) describes the essential role of the teacher: "Surely, nothing can be more important than finding the source of learning, not in extrinsic demand, but in human freedom" (p. 132). The ability to find ones' individual singing tone or consistency in singing is not inherent; it is not an ability that naturally exists. It must be discovered by the student, guided by an effective voice instructor through an exploration of freedom.

An existentialist framework for vocal instruction, such as that considered in this research study, may offer the instructor and student a glimpse of the possibilities. Greene declares, "Art offers life; it offers hope; it offers the prospect of discovery; it offers light" (1995, p. 133). A voice instructor may have the opportunity to define her essence as a facilitator of voice study and to possibly alter her facticity as an instructor. If many of her students are unable to sing with consistency and an emotional connection, perhaps self-reflection and a way to reconsider her teaching approach, such as that offered in an existentialist framework, may alter this facticity. I believe using an existentialist approach for vocal instruction may discern ways to help a student discover hope, art, and an artistic and emotional experience in singing.

CONCLUSION

Existentialism has informed education practice to offer alternative ways of considering the student as an individual. It provides a view of the student-teacher relationship that strives to inspire individuality and responsibility in learning, leading to students who have independence, autonomy, and an ability to choose and find freedom. The key principles that underpin existentialism and its application to education are instructing the individual with flexibility, making the student aware of free will and responsibility, while at the same time helping the student face feelings of abandonment and anguish. A student-teacher relationship based in existentialism offers the ability for both teacher and student to find each one's essence. It puts the individual in charge of what she will become. It offers choice for both teacher and student. The teacher can choose to find her essence as a teacher. Existentialism offers the ability of choice; a teacher does not have to feel trapped in using just one teaching approach or one way of approaching students. Free will can be used to give the teacher an opportunity to choose from a variety of teaching tools to help address the individual student.

These existentialist ideas may also be considered in re-conceptualizing the student-teacher relationship in the voice studio and may inform vocal pedagogy practice. A voice instructor may consider such Sartrean principles as freedom, free will, choice, and responsibility, and may have the opportunity to help student mitigate inconsistency in singing. If a teacher has an acute awareness of her responsibility, combined with knowledge of many pedagogical approaches to vocal instruction geared towards teaching the individual, using her free will to choose an approach can perhaps provide a way to mitigate inconsistency in her students. Once a student has gained an awareness of how to sing consistently, she has independence and autonomy, and may have an ability to use her free will to make individual artistic choices in interpreting music. One that is not distracted by inconsistent singing has a world of possibilities in front of her. The aim is for voice students to become engaged in a piece of music and make unique choices that are expressive of themselves. The voice teacher using an existentialist framework for instructing has an opportunity to create her essence as a teacher, and to become the type of teacher that has students that are able to give consistent, artistic and free performances.

This chapter showed the use of existentialist principles as a beneficial foundation for general education. I have examined how these principles may inform vocal instruction in higher education. The next chapter will describe how a phenomenological framework for studying the effectiveness of an existentialist approach in vocal instruction is an appropriate choice for this study. As well, I will outline the methods of data collection that will be used in keeping with a phenomenological study.

CHAPTER 4

Hermeneutic Phenomenology and Existentialism

INTRODUCTION

The purpose of my research was to develop a deeper understanding of the student-teacher relationship and to consider ways that pedagogues can facilitate more consistent and emotional singing and further, can explore their own essence as voice instructors. This study explored ways to attempt to mitigate these issues through a student-teacher relationship influenced by the existentialist principles of Sartre as a way to consider vocal instruction holistically or, in other words, instruct the voice student in all aspects of singing. It describes a complete approach that attempts to address all elements of obtaining consistency in singing as well as addressing the mind, emotions, and experience of the student to facilitate emotional engagement. In this chapter, I outline the hermeneutic phenomenological framework that I used to orient my research methodology and, following this, I detail the research method I employed for this study.

EXISTENTIALISM AND A HERMENEUTIC PHENOMENOLOGICAL FRAMEWORK

A methodology based in phenomenology complemented the existential theoretical framework for this research study. Sartre's existentialism was not a pure form of existentialism but rather a fusion of existentialism and phenomenology, and thus this methodological approach is fitting (Merleau-Ponty, 1962, 1969; Sartre, 2001; van Manen, 1984, 1990). Grounding the theoretical framework of a teaching approach based in existentialist thought and using a phenomenological framework for my methods enabled me to ascertain if a teaching approach influenced by Sartre's existentialist principles was effective. I was able to gain insight into the experience of the student participants and determine whether or not they considered a teaching method based in existentialist thought helped them find consistency in singing and a means to explore creativity in singing. A phenomenological study offered ways to present a view of the student experience in vocal study. [23]

Phenomenology is the appearance of things, or things as they appear in our experience, and the ways in which we experience things. Thus, of the meaning's things have in our experience, phenomenology asks, "What is this or that kind of experience like?" (van Manen, 1990, pg. 9). The concept of phenomenology or a "lived experience" is related to consciousness and awareness, described as being-for-itself in the existentialist overview of Sartre. This experience was considered in reference to the act and art of vocal instruction and singing.

The act of singing is a phenomenon and an experience. Singers are the instruments through which music and the sensation of their individual voices are experienced. It is a blind activity, so one must rely upon and interpret consistency based on physical feedback, kinesthetic awareness, observation, and detailed descriptions such as those found in phenomenological studies. The existentialist idea of being-for-itself, as Sartre describes it, involves consciousness and awareness. An existentialist framework, as well as a phenomenological methodology, provided an opportunity to interpret consistency and emotional engagement in singing through considering experience and a change in consciousness and awareness. This was done through an interpretation of the students' consciousness and awareness of their instruments, of their emotional engagement in music, and through a determination of whether they believed this teaching approach was effective or not in guiding them to find artistic freedom while being responsible in the learning process. As well, the awareness and consciousness of the vocal instructor was considered in gauging any change in consistency and emotional engagement in singing.

Phenomenological research also provides the opportunity to "borrow other people's experience and their reflection on their experiences" (van Manen, 1990, p. 62).

In this study, as I will illustrate further in the Methods section, I attempted to borrow the experience of the students and to interpret their experience as a way to consider whether or not attempting an existentialist framework for vocal instruction is beneficial in helping to mitigate inconsistent and unemotional singing by higher education students, and if it may be offered for consideration in higher education voice studios and for pre-service voice instructors.

---

[23] I have consciously chosen to use the word "student" instead of "participant" in the methodology portion of this paper, as the central aim of this dissertation is to bring to the forefront a humanistic approach to education and vocal instruction.

The student-teacher relationship in the voice studio is also one of experience. The instructor witnesses and experiences the student while singing. This is through the experience of hearing and sensing the student's voice and, if this instructor is effective, she may have the opportunity to interpret the student's experience through an acute awareness of whether or not the student is singing with consistency and if she understands the information being facilitated regarding vocal technique. As well, the instructor has the unique experience of an aesthetic reaction to the student singing through which she senses whether the student is emotionally engaged or not. With this in mind, a hermeneutic phenomenological study was an appropriate orientation to consider any changes in student consistency and emotional engagement and to determine whether or not this teaching approach may be considered effective.

Phenomenological research offers ways to question how one experiences something. For this study, it offered for interpretation a way for the voice student to express her experiences and reaction to being instructed with a teaching approach influenced by Sartre's existentialist principles. As well, it offered a way to consider if this teaching approach is effective or not in guiding consistent and emotional singing through interpretation of the student experience, as well as expressing my own interpretation and experience of any change in consistency and emotional engagement. According to van Manen (1990), hermeneutic phenomenology, "is a human science which studies persons" (p. 6). Phenomenological research literature allows that the researcher has a personal interest in the research (Gadamer, 1977; Moustakas, 1994; Regan, 2012; van Manen, 1990), and such was the case in this study. I have a great deal of personal interest in this research. As stated in my identification of the problem for this study, I frequently experience inconsistent and unemotional singing by students in voice lessons, voice juries, competitions, recitals, and master classes. As a vocal pedagogue and performing artist, my personal interest is to help students mitigate this problem. I believe the source is a teaching problem and that perhaps many pre-service teachers are not obtaining tools to instruct the complete student as an individual in ways that can facilitate consistency and emotional engagement in music. As well, many currently practicing instructors with performance degrees are typically not taught how to teach, and perhaps they are left attempting to instruct in the approach with which they were instructed or are attempting other approaches without guidance or feedback. Some voice instructors may be wonderful performers and artists; however, they may not have obtained a set of teaching tools that are effective to facilitate consistency and artistry in their students. As well, some instructors may feel they are restricted in using just one or two approaches. I have a great deal of interest in offering ways for voice instructors to consider how important their role is in the voice studio and the responsibility they have in instructing voice in higher education. My personal interest in this research study was motivated by a wish to offer instructors ways to consider or reconsider how voice is instructed. In presenting a theoretical framework grounded in existentialist thought, I hope that I may offer instructors a way to consider effective vocal instruction and, perhaps, I can help mitigate inconsistent and unengaged singing in students.

Hermeneutics offers a way to uncover and to interpret a lived experience. An orientation blending both is called hermeneutic phenomenology. This provides a way for the researcher to consider and have attentiveness towards what he or she may take for granted or assume in a research study. This approach gives one a view of the actual experience of a participant or individual. With this awareness and insight, one has the opportunity to explore the lived experience of an individual or individuals. Using this approach for this study presents the opportunity for me to gain insight, to reflect upon, and interpret the experience of the students instructed using existentialist principles. Examining the student-teacher relationship in the voice studio is an interpretation of pedagogy. Pedagogy is "the activity of teaching, parenting, educating" (van Manen, 1990, p. 2). A hermeneutic phenomenological framework gives a researcher the opportunity to describe and interpret the lived experience of a concept with several individuals who have shared an experience and the notion that "pedagogy requires a phenomenological sensitivity to lived experience" (p. 2). Hermeneutic phenomenology studies humans and their experiences in the world. This means positioning oneself to view the experience of individuals while interpreting their experience and reaction to this lived experience. Both the interpretation of the students' experience and my interpretation of changes in consistency and emotional engagement are relevant for this study, as the role of the voice instructor in the student-teacher relationship is essential. If the instructor is effective, she may have the ability to guide her student to technical consistency and thus foster artistic freedom and an emotional connection to music in students. The way to ascertain if this method grounded in existentialist thought is helpful to students and an approach for consideration for voice instructors is to view this experience both from the descriptive personal perspective of the student and from the interpretation of her experience from a distance, as was the case in this study (the methods for data collection and interpretation will be detailed in the Methods section).

Hermeneutic phenomenological research can also be considered the study and interpretation of essence and experience. It is a way to approach research that can help the researcher come to a deeper understanding of an individual's experience when exposed to or as part of a phenomenon. Researchers gain insight into the choices and decisions that stem from this experience determining one's essence. An individual in existentialist thought makes choices to determine her essence or her outcome. These choices create an experience for the individual. Experiences can cause reflection, a kinesthetic awareness, and perhaps a deeper realization of one's existence in the present moment. In this study, I had the opportunity to examine the student experience in being instructed with a teaching approach guided by existentialist principles. I interpreted the students' experiences and observed changes in their consistent singing and emotional engagement in singing through evaluating aesthetic responses. Their experience led to self-reflection, both by the students and by me, as the instructor. As well, the study provided an opportunity for a deeper understanding in the student-teacher relationship in our voice studio. I developed a deeper awareness of responsibility and a realization that the choices one makes determines outcome and essence through a lived experience of these choices and explorations.

In phenomenological studies, phenomenological reductions take place in which a summary of the meanings or themes that emerge from interviews and reflective journals occurs. This reduction takes place while *bracketing* as much of the researcher's personal interpretation as possible. This process is also known as *epoché* (Husserl in Smith, 1995; Hycner, 1985, Moustakas, 1994; van Manen, 1990). A phenomenological reduction is the process by which a researcher opens herself up to the meaning of the information presented in interviews or journal entries. Bracketing or *epoché* is an attempt to suspend; to not interpret data from the researcher's point of view, and to try to describe the participant's experience as accurately as possible. I attempted to bracket as much of my personal opinion as I could.

In the field of arts and aesthetics in education, Elliot Eisner (1976, 1985, 2002) describes methods of evaluation that are available to assess aesthetic response. Such is the case in the phenomenon of singing, as a performance is an aesthetic and phenomenological experience to which one will have an aesthetic response if the student is emotionally engaged. Emotional engagement cannot be measured empirically or by a standardized test or survey. The aesthetic response of an expert, such as I provided, is necessary as a way to evaluate whether or not a performance is emotionally engaged. Eisner (1985) speaks of *educational connoisseurship*, stating, "To be a connoisseur of anything—wine, bicycles or graphic arts— is to be informed about their qualities" (p. 92). Such an approach is attentive to an appreciation of what one encounters aesthetically, not in the sense that one likes what one hears or sees, but rather in terms of an informed awareness of or response to the experience. It is a valued tool of qualitative assessment in the field of arts.

Harold Osborne (1991) writes of how one engages in aesthetic assessment by noting the presence of artistic excellence and aesthetic satisfaction. For the purpose of this study, it will be said that a student displaying consistency and emotional engagement in performances will exhibit a certain level of artistic excellence and will elicit an aesthetic response from her audience.

Osborne (1991) speaks of *stature*. He describes stature as displaying a high level of competence and the ability to elicit responses such as non-verbal thought or a reaction, whether positive or negative, to a piece or art or music. An additional aesthetic response Osborne describes is emotional quality; that is, the depth of the emotional reaction one has to a piece of art, whether it is an abstract painting, a poem, or music. The qualitative tools of assessment described provide a way to evaluate data obtained from videotaped lessons and performance as a way to measure any change in consistency and emotional engagement in performance.

Educational research provides the opportunity to examine pedagogic practice and offers ways to re-focus or re-conceptualize thought. In considering a hermeneutic phenomenological orientation for a study, it is necessary to frame the question to be studied, "the phenomenon that the researcher seeks to illuminate" (Osborne, 1990, p. 79). This framework presents the opportunity to examine the individual (in this case the voice student), her teacher and their relationship—and perhaps offer a way to facilitate consistency and emotional engagement in singing through the realization of individual freedom and responsibility.

The very nature of a framework grounded in existentialism and hermeneutic phenomenology is a symbiotic approach to consider. One must understand and interpret the essence and experience participants have while engaging in the study (Gadamer, 1977; Laverty, 2003; Merleau-Ponty, 1962, 1969, 1992; Olivares, Peterson & Hess, 2007; Regan, 2012; van Manen, 1990, 2007). As researcher in this hermeneutic phenomenological study, I acted as "a sensitive observer to the subtleties of everyday life....as they pertain to his or her domain of interest" (van Manen, 1990). In this case, I discovered a way to observe and interpret the student experience in a course of vocal study influenced by several of Sartre's existentialist principles.

THE RESEARCH METHOD FOR THIS STUDY

A framework grounded in hermeneutic phenomenology offers a way to interpret the students' reflective journals detailing both their experience in the process of this study and their opinion of the teaching approach (Gadamer, 1977; Moustakas, 1994; Regan, 2012; van Manen, 1990). The aim was to explore how students experienced their essence as singers and performers and, specifically, how singers experienced the process of singing consistently and while emotionally engaged. In this research study, I explored the essence of the individual and attempted to view changes in the students' essence, both in their own perception of their essence as a singer and in my interpretation, through detailed descriptions of their experience as well as interpretation of data. I positioned myself as a researcher, an insider, and an artist-teacher. Positioning myself as an insider allowed me to reflect upon my own aesthetic experience while watching the students perform (Herr & Anderson, 2005). The students in this study were instructed in voice in a manner that attempted to encourage them to explore their freedom and to face responsibility in existentialist terms. My hope for this study was for the students to find consistency in singing and the opportunity to explore their freedom when guided by my instruction towards awareness and consciousness in vocal study.

Three students from the ages of eighteen to thirty years of age were purposefully selected. I selected students with various voice types, at various levels of vocal development, and from various backgrounds in terms of vocal ability. I selected a first-year music student from my higher education voice studio, a mezzo-soprano, as a participant. She was new to higher education vocal studies. She had engaged in private voice lessons focusing on classical repertoire for several years prior to entering the music program at the university. Her lessons did not entail a great deal of vocal technique, nor did they include much instruction in expressive singing. The second student participant, a soprano, was a second-year student from my studio engaged in vocal studies at the university. This student had just over one year of vocal study at the higher education level in my studio prior to entering this study. Prior to her first year of higher education vocal studies, her primary focus was in musical theatre singing, whereas the focus in higher education for our university is on classical repertoire. Working with this student gave me the opportunity to fine tune the teaching approach that I began to use with her in her first year of the music program by narrowing the focus of my vocal instruction to a theoretical framework clearly based in existentialist principles. It also presented me with the opportunity to gauge progress or regression in her vocal development when instructed with an existentialist framework as my foundation. Finally, the third student participant was a new student to my Conservatory voice studio. She was an adult student, who worked full time in a job completely unrelated to music. She was a non-university student interested in vocal development, and an individual who was primarily a choral singer prior to participating in this study. I thought it would be interesting and relevant to gauge her development and experience in this study in comparison to the students fully immersed in a higher education music program. Each student was quite different from the others. Including this diversity of students as participants presented a way to determine if the teaching method is applicable and helpful for a variety of students engaged in vocal study.

The study cycle was a school term of approximately sixteen weeks. All students were female, as I used current students as participants, and I did not have any male students in my studio. I instructed two undergraduate music students in higher education majoring in voice, in addition to one conservatory student in the approximately same age range not enrolled in a university music program, as a way to compare and interpret the students' development and experience.

Video analysis, interviews, audio recordings, and reflective journals were used to capture the experience of these students (Gadamer, 1977; Regan,

2012; van Manen, 1984, 1990; Weber, 1986). Lessons were videotaped approximately one time per month to gauge changes. I noted changes in the level of consistent singing, breath support, physical tension, clarity of tone, and posture, as well as changes in emotional engagement in performance. Public performances were videotaped approximately one time per month to monitor change and to gauge the student's ability to give emotionally engaged and connected, as well as technically consistent, performances. Video analysis was very valuable as a means to gain insight for a hermeneutic interpretation of the students' experience in this study (Flick, 2009; Hatch, 2002; Heath, Hindmarsh & Luff, 2010; Moustakas, 1994; Spiers, 2004; van Manen, 1990). It helped me view the performance and to reflect upon and interpret whether or not singers were engaged or "in the moment." As well, it was a way to closely monitor posture and any indication of physical tension. Videos of the students also offered a way for me to aesthetically experience the students' performances, to gauge their emotional engagement, and to decide whether there was a change in these or not (Herr & Anderson, 2005).

As I mentioned in the previous section, my expertise lies in vocal instruction, vocal performance, and pedagogy, and so I am qualified to provide expert analysis and interpretation of the video materials (Eisner, 1976, 1985, 2002; Osborne, 1991). The way in which I interpreted the video data initially was to make notes on the characteristics of each student at the beginning of the study. I determined her depth of emotional engagement in performance and in lessons, as well as recording specific details of all aspects of her vocal consistency and development at the onset of the study. This set a baseline from which I could interpret any changes in consistency or emotional engagement in performance and lessons, and offered a way to compare how the students experienced singing in lessons and performances, both the parallels and the differences among them. I saved each video in chronological order to interpret changes throughout the course of the study and noted instances where students made progress or lacked progress. This valuable visual and audio information gave me additional layers of materials to consider when extracting themes. It presented ways for me to consider the students' experience by interpreting their body language and the engagement in their eyes during lessons and performance, as well functioning as a means to interpret development in consistency in singing. This material was beneficial, in that it provided another view into the experience of the students in addition to other materials collected.

Weekly interviews with the students took place during lessons to record weekly progress and to discuss their weekly experience in practice sessions and other singing experiences (Moustakas, 1994; Smith, 1995; van Manen, 1990; Weber, 1986). These weekly interviews offered the opportunity to assess how the students experienced vocal study and to discover if they felt they gained independence and autonomy while practicing. Weekly interviews during lessons and talking to the students informally about their experience also provided me with the opportunity to be flexible. I could then adjust how I facilitated each student individually to attempt to ensure that she was gaining consistency in singing; thus, I could attempt to lead the students to explore artistic freedom.

The students were asked to engage in reflective journaling while being instructed with this pedagogical method, so that they could accurately describe their experience in being instructed with this teaching approach (Groenewald, 2004; Laverty, 2003; Moustakas, 1994; van Manen, 1990). As well, students were asked to evaluate the teaching approach through their journaling, to offer their opinions and views of whether it was effective or not. They were asked to give detailed descriptions of their own experience in being instructed with existentialist principles as a teaching framework.

There was a documentary analysis reviewing books and articles as well as web-based sources by voice instructors, performers, researchers of vocal pedagogy, and researchers in educational philosophy. These included existential writings, in particular those of and about Sartre. Documentary analysis provided a way to perform a thematic analysis (Bowen, 2009; Moustakas, 1994; van Manen, 1984, 1990). Bowen (2009) indicates:

> It is not a matter of lining up a series of excerpts from printed material to convey whatever idea comes to the researcher's mind. Rather, it is a process of evaluating documents in such a way that empirical knowledge is produced, and understanding is developed. (p.33)

This analysis was of considerable value to this study as a way to examine teaching approaches and to analyze some of the principles of Sartre in order to re-cast my teaching method.

With the value of documentary analysis apparent, I reviewed further dissertations and articles about vocal performance, teaching voice, the psychology of teaching, philosophical and existentialist approaches to teaching, as well as those using a humanistic approach to teaching in general education. I performed this review and analysis so that I might gain a deeper understanding of voice teaching practices, the existentialist principles of Sartre, and existential approaches to teaching and education theory. Mogalakwe (2006) notes that "the documentary research method should be utilised by social scientists with the full confidence that it is also a respected scientific method" (p. 229). Further understanding of current teaching emphasis in vocal pedagogy and existentialist principles provided me with the opportunity to use the theoretical framework described in the previous chapter to theorize about and elaborate on existing research about existential teaching by applying it specifically to vocal instruction.

Themes emerged showing changes in consistency and changes in the ability to sing independently, as the students' experiences were interpreted for potential evidence of freedom in artistic performance (Barritt, Beekman, Bleeker & Mulderij, 1984; Moustakas, 1994; van Manen, 1990). In phenomenological research, one uses themes to attempt to identify the elements of what makes up an experience. This was relevant and beneficial for a research study of vocal instruction, as the opportunity was presented to identify which aspects (elements) of vocal technique, independence, autonomy, consistency, and emotional engagement, responsibility, and freedom exhibited change. This paradigm of research allowed me as well to consider and evaluate whether certain aspects of vocal technique can be facilitated with this teaching approach, leading to effective changes in breath or awareness of resonance, for example.

Drawing upon the notion of bracketing and *epoché*, I undertook a phenomenological reduction to find emerging themes and interpreted their meaning, relating this back to my identified problem and research questions. I positioned myself as an expert or connoisseur in vocal instruction and performance, while attempting to liberate myself from preconceived bias. To help suspend my bias, I returned to the students with results for an additional interview as a validity check to ensure that their experience was accurately described. As well, the reflective-interpretive nature of a hermeneutic phenomenological study allowed me to correct prejudgment in this process, while I attempted to accurately interpret the experience described in the students' reflective journals. The video and audio recording of performances presented me with the means to interpret changes in consistency and emotions that may not have been reflected in the journal entries of the students.

Once this reduction of themes took place and as much of the experience as was possible to describe was written, I further interpreted students' experience in lessons and performance recordings in relation to my research question, attempting to determine whether applying Sartre's principles to a teaching method positively affected or changed consistency and emotional engagement in singing or not. Narrative descriptions, as opposed to tables, of the emergent themes were used to capture the nature of the students' experiences.

The next section will outline the limitations of this study.

Limitations

This section will provide information on the limitations of this particular research study. The method for choosing participants from my own voice studio may be considered a limitation. The nature of higher education voice studios would not allow me to borrow a student from another teacher's studio while she was engaged in vocal study during the university term. The purpose of the study was to gain insight into the experience of higher education vocal study and provide detailed analysis of how suitably Sartre's principles might influence the student-teacher relationship in the voice studio. Using students from my own studio provided the opportunity to interpret the students' experience in great detail. There is a high level of trust in the voice studio and choosing my own students as participants served to obtain the most authentic descriptions of the student experience in this study. There was a thorough consideration of the student participants' well-being by the ethics review board for this study. The nature of the end of term voice exams at my institution—in addition to the fact that all four voice faculty members were present at the exams, although the studio teacher was not allowed to grade her own students— assured the ethics review board that no student would experience any level of risk-taking part in this study.

Another limitation considered was that all students were female. This is because there are a limited number of male students in higher education voice programs in general, and at my institution we had only two enrolled, neither of whom were part of my voice studio. As a way to mitigate this limitation, I selected diverse female participants to try to gain insight into the effectiveness of this teaching approach as it would translate to all types of students.

Student illness was also a limitation in this study. As the body is an instrument, at the times during the research study that students became ill, they were not able to sing. The after-effects of a cold or flu are experienced by singers for many days. This affected the progress of some of the students, as they had to reestablish consistency in singing and therefore had minor setbacks in development. As well, feeling ill affected the students' ability to sing with emotion. If one is feeling sick with a sore throat and headache, for example, this presents a challenge to think about emotions and expressivity.

Performance nerves and anxiety were also limitations. Some students experienced nerves in performance, which affected their ability to sing consistently and with emotional engagement, although they had gained some consistency and emotional awareness in practice and in lessons. It was noted that the students who experienced some nerves in public performance, although well prepared, also indicated that they experienced nerves and anxiety in other situations in which a high level of competency was expected: taking exams, giving class presentations, and in piano and sight-singing exams in their other classes at the university.

Another consideration in this study was the students' self-esteem. Singing is a very personal activity and is one in which a student can often feel quite vulnerable. I believe that some were more comfortable than others with themselves in general, and that this caused the students to each have a different experience in this study.

Uncovering Students' Experience While Singing

In this study, several themes were revealed through an interpretation of the reflective journals, interview recordings, and the review of the video footage of participants' performances. I attempted to uncover the most accurate view of the students' experience and give them the opportunity to express their opinions, experiences, and feedback on this teaching approach, guiding them to detach any personal reflections on me as their instructor. I reassured them that the reflections—any positive, constructive, or negative feedback—and their views and descriptions of their experiences were very valuable and necessary to determine if this teaching approach based in existentialist principles was a beneficial approach for them.

My hermeneutic phenomenological reflection began in January 2013. I describe this as a reflection rather than a data analysis, as I wish to consider a humanistic approach to vocal instruction and reflection on the materials obtained in this study. As well, using a teaching approach based in the existentialist principles of responsibility and freedom caused a great deal of reflection in me. I reflected continuously on each student's progress, their weekly interviews, the performances, and the questions they brought to lessons. I reflected on ways to approach them to address each student's individualised needs.

I instructed three voices students, as I described in my methodology. I will give each student a pseudonym for the purpose of anonymity as indicated in my ethics approval and by the consent of the participants. The first student I called *Alexandra*, the second student *Katherine*, and the third, *Nina*. I instructed the three voice students, creating a student-teacher relationship with a theoretical framework based in the existentialist principles of responsibility and freedom at its very center. I viewed each student in this study as a blank slate, full of potential and possibilities. Although the students had a history of some vocal study, I considered each student as an individual, viewing them with a clean slate, working from the foundation where they presented themselves to me in my voice studio. I faced my responsibility as a facilitator of voice and took on the task of instructing each student as an individual in a humanistic manner. This entailed giving instruction and attempting to guide each student to make discoveries about their voices and themselves as singers. I explored my freedom as an individual and an instructor to consider and chose from numerous approaches in vocal instruction to guide each student. I used a very flexible approach, depending on what problem each student presented at her weekly lesson. I attempted to instill a sense of responsibility in each student, encouraging her to become a stakeholder in her vocal development, and leading her towards independence, autonomy and consistent singing. In this sense, I used a "no excuses" approach to instruction, making the students aware that they were ultimately responsible for their own outcome as singers and performers. Though I was the guide and facilitator, each of them had to face responsibility and take an active role in developing her instrument. This notion is based in Sartre's (2007) principles of responsibility and freedom. We, as individuals, are charged with determining our outcome in the world and what we will become.

I attempted to guide the students to find consistency in vocal technique through the influence of Sartre's principles. In working towards leading the students to gain responsibility, I also attempted to lead them to explore and find freedom. In guiding the students to vocal consistency, I hoped to help them emotionally engage in singing and thus explore freedom. I guided the students to find physical freedom in singing, as well as to explore artistic freedom, by fostering ways for them to interpret and emotionally connect to the vocal music they studied during the term. I also attempted to foster freedom in guiding them to explore their essence and attempted to make them aware that they determined their own essence as singers through choice. I worked to instill the knowledge that they had the ability to make choices that defined their essence as singers.

In order to gain insight, to explore and to interpret the students' experience while being instructed with this approach, I collected materials of their lived experience. At the start of the university term or research cycle, I began to ask guiding questions in our interviews at the onset of weekly lessons, leading to discussions about how the students experienced their voices and the teaching approach during practice sessions each week. This gave me a great deal of insight into to what challenges they encountered in finding vocal consistency and whether or not they were facing their responsibility in vocal development and study. If, for example, a student mentioned that she had a lot of school work or assignments and didn't have much time to practice, this gave me an indication that she was not facing responsibility. I was then able to address and uncover the reasons for this and work to address them immediately by reminding the student that she determined her outcome. These interviews were recorded.

The three students were asked to begin writing a reflective journal at the beginning of the term. I requested that they reflect upon and write about their practice sessions, lessons, and performances in order to present a view of their experience in this approach towards vocal study, as "writing forces the person into a reflective attitude" (van Manen, 1990, p. 64). I attempted to understand their personal experience while engaged in this study. In researching lived experience, I looked for the participants to describe the experience as they "live it" and asked them to describe the experience from "the inside," and to be attentive and aware. With this in mind, I asked the students to reflect and write on their experience in being instructed with my teaching approach based in existentialist thought. I asked the students to offer me, as the reader, a view of their personal experience, as well as an assessment or opinion of the teaching approach, and to express whether they believed the approach was beneficial or not in helping find consistency in singing and an ability to emotionally engage. My hope was that the students' reflective journals would give me a view into their lived experience and raise self-assessment and motivation in the students to practice and reflect at a deeper level during their practice and lessons. (I hoped to instill responsibility through this task as well). I gave the students some questions or reflective prompts to consider throughout the course of the research study and asked them to write their thoughts, feelings, and experiences in the reflective journals. Questions or reflective prompts included:

- What were the technical challenges you often faced in the practice room?
- Did this teaching method help you mitigate these challenges and/or help you find a better awareness of your instrument, leading to consistency or not?
- Did you feel you gained and faced responsibility for yourself and for your instrument's development while being instructed with this teaching approach or not?
- Did you feel I faced my responsibility as a facilitator of vocal instruction or not? Were you instructed in a way that showed I was engaged and a stakeholder in your vocal development or did I not show engagement?
- Did you feel you were instructed with an individualised approach addressing your specific needs or not?
- Did you experience freedom (physical freedom, an ability to choose, artistic freedom) while being instructed with this teaching approach?
- Did you face feelings of fear, anguish, and abandonment? Did you find ways to deal with these feelings through this teaching approach?
- Did you experience holistic instruction? Were all aspects being addressed (technical aspects, mind, body, spirit, emotions, and experience)?

The responses to these reflective prompts, as well as the students' journal entries, weekly lesson interviews, and videos of performances gave a valuable view of their experience and helped uncover some themes.

Identification of the Themes That Emerged

In an attempt to unearth the essence of the experience of the students and to uncover themes, I began to consider the responses and reflective writing from the student journals, as well as the audio and video materials of the students. I looked for ways to access and to uncover the experience of the students. I reflected upon and interpreted the connections of the materials collected to my research question, asking to what extent Sartre's existentialist principles of responsibility and freedom suitably influenced the student-teacher relationship I created in my voice studio. Reviewing performance videos gave me the opportunity to consider if using these principles as a theoretical framework helped to improve inconsistency and lack of emotional engagement in the students, and if these principles guided students to face responsibility, to explore, and to find freedom in singing and artistry. Phenomenological hermeneutic reflection allowed me to uncover, identify and interpret some themes in reviewing the material for this study. I discovered the following themes. It is beyond the scope of this study to extract the many other numerous themes that may exist. I will depict the large themes and then give a detailed narrative of each theme and their connection to my research question:

> To what extent can Jean-Paul Sartre's existentialist principles of responsibility and freedom suitably influence the student-teacher relationship and be applied to vocal development to improve inconsistent and emotionally unengaged singing in undergraduate music students?

At the very core of these themes are the principles of responsibility and freedom. These principles were central to the themes, the teaching approach, and the discoveries of both the students and me. In the following chapter, I will give detailed narratives on each theme and how each connects to the principles of responsibility and freedom. As well, I will explain their influence on the student-teacher relationship and if they fostered a change in consistency and emotional engagement in the students, and eventually lead both the students and me to the realization of what we can become. The next chapter will show the findings and will include an analysis with reference to Sartre's existentialist principles of responsibility and freedom.

CHAPTER 5

Freedom and Responsibility of the Singer

In this study, I examined my student-teacher relationships in the voice studio with the specific intent of considering how Sartre's principles of responsibility and freedom may help to mitigate inconsistency and a lack of emotional engagement in voice students in higher education. As I aimed to foster students' increasing sense of their own responsibility and freedom as vocalists, the process highlighted emerging themes: awareness, resistance, fear, acceptance, and becoming. In the following sections, I will clarify how Sartre's view of the human condition helped influence my teaching approach and led students to find more responsibility and freedom in vocal development with an improvement in vocal consistency and an ability to engage emotionally with music and text.

AWARENESS

Two aspects of awareness were prevalent during the vocal instruction. In this chapter, I begin with the explanation of how the theme of awareness of my responsibility influenced the student-teacher relationship in my voice studio with the student participants, and I then analyse the students' self-awareness of responsibility.

I introduced Sartre's (2007) principle of responsibility to each student, considering his words "man is responsible" (p. 23). I first had to examine my role in the student-teacher relationship and consider my own responsibility. I reflected on passages about Sartre's (2007) view of the individual's responsibility for her existence, in that she is responsible for what she is and what she will ultimately become. I became aware that I must accept the reality that I was my own project, that I must define the type of instructor I would be for the students engaged in this study, and that I must understand the implications that this would have on my teaching practice in terms of defining my essence as instructor. I also considered the notion of responsibility and determined that I would have to make the students aware that they were also their own project the sum of their choices and decisions. Their vocal development, and how ultimately successful or improved it was, would be in their hands, would be their responsibility. I believed this would be a beneficial foundation for establishing our roles in the student-teacher relationship influenced by Sartre's existentialist thought. I would be the guide and facilitator, the one who was responsible for each student; in turn, each student would also need to recognize that she too would be responsible.

In considering how I could be a more effective instructor and guide, I also considered Sartre's idea that, in taking on responsibility for myself, I would also be taking on the responsibility for others— in this case, my students. In so doing, I became very aware of my responsibility as the guide for each student. Given Sartre's (1984) emphasis that individuals should be viewed ontologically as a blank state, I started with that premise, and considered how I could attend to each student in helping her find emotional engagement and consistency through her own independence. I believed that this would be a beneficial way to position myself as a more effective instructor. In viewing each student as a blank slate, I considered the notion central to Sartre's (Ibid) thinking, the notion that one exists prior to creating one's essence. Viewing each student as existing and being aware that each student had a past and that perhaps her own ideas of how she should be instructed might emerge, I reflected upon how this development could affect our relationship. If a student was taught in a rote manner before, for example, perhaps she would find my teaching approach, instilling responsibility and leading to an exploration of freedom, challenging. In aligning my teaching approach with Sartre's tenet, however, I used the notion that the past was a passive place for each student. I became aware that I had to begin in the present in order to determine my essence as an effective instructor and to find ways to guide the students to determine their outcome in finding consistency and emotions in singing. Just as I had to consider that each student was beginning as a blank slate, I also had to view the way I instructed the students as a new beginning. This was a way to re-examine and reconsider my teaching approach to recast it in Sartrean terms.

The repositioning of my teaching approach also occurred when considering the notion of being-for-itself as described by Sartre (1984) as influencing my teaching approach. Being-for-itself is centered in consciousness and awareness in relation to the individual. I had to be conscious and aware to see if my teaching approach was effective. As well, I set the goal in our lessons to guide the students to be conscious and aware of their instruments and how to use them consistently. Further, I had to make them conscious of the importance of being fully responsible for themselves. This explicit notion of responsibility was to influence how they would work on finding their individual singing tone.

In order to find this tone, one must be fully conscious of what is happening in the body. This is kinesthetic awareness. Kinesthetic awareness means that the student is fully physically and mentally conscious and is aware of how to use her instrument; in other words, she has complete ownership of her voice. If, for example, a student is mindlessly singing repetitive exercises without focus or with a goal in mind, she is not fully conscious of her instrument and will likely not find consistency. As I reflected upon my role in the student-teacher relationship, a vivid awareness of my responsibility to foster consciousness and awareness in the students emerged. I made each student aware of her role in our relationship at our first session, letting her know that although I was the guide and facilitator, my expectation was that ultimately, she would be responsible in determining whether or not she would find consistency in singing. I wanted to instill this awareness of responsibility in each student as well as work with each student to lead her to discover an individual awareness of her instrument. This teaching tenet was grounded in Sartre's (2007) principle of responsibility.

The theme of awareness of responsibility from the students emerged from our discussions at the beginning of the study, and their reaction to it was reflected in the journals. I let each student know that I would be the guide through the process of her self-discovery. As well, I believe that I made them aware that I would help them make connections to find their individual resonant vocal tone. I let them know we would work collaborate to help ensure that they could access this tone consistency and that we would work towards building a foundation upon which they could explore aspects of freedom in singing. I also let them know that I expected independent work from each student. I informed the students that there were expectations: that students had to be responsible, had to be prepared, must work to experiment with the ideas we talked about in lessons, and must try to build muscle memory. As well, I let them know that they must attempt to be conscious and focused when practicing. Each student felt that I faced my responsibility in our relationship. It was also clear that I made them acutely aware that they too had responsibilities in our student-teacher relationship. I believe that in this aspect I was able to instill knowledge and an expectation of responsibility in the students as well as face my own responsibility as their facilitator. The students agreed that I had made them aware of their role in our student-teacher relationship and in their own development. I asked them to look back on our study in a reflective prompt, and to reveal if they felt were encouraged to take on responsibility in our relationship; each student did feel that she was encouraged to be responsible. Nina wrote, "I absolutely feel you have encouraged me to be responsible in my vocal study and you encouraged independence" (Nina, Reflective Journal, April 18, 2013). Nina was clearly aware that I wanted her to be responsible in her study and outcome. Katherine experienced awareness of responsibility, stating, "I was made aware to take on this responsibility, as I wanted to be prepared and improved" (Katherine, Reflective Journal, April 20, 2013). I interpret Katherine's post as awareness of my expectations about her responsibility of being an active part of her vocal development in our student-teacher relationship. This is not to be confused with strictness, as it was made clear to the students that they were to be responsible for themselves, and that the approach was not about strictness but rather about instilling a sense of ownership and an active role in the process of each student's vocal development. Alexandra's reaction to learning was that she was to be fully responsible for her part in her vocal development as well as her outcome was quite positive. She wrote, "I was encouraged to take responsibility for my vocal studies in terms of practicing and vocal health" (Alexandra, Reflective Journal, April 19, 2013). In this passage, Alexandra revealed that she was made aware of her role in our student-teacher relationship and that I wanted her to be responsible for her development, as well as aware of how to take care of her instrument. I determined that responsibility is central to defining essence; one must first become aware of one's responsibility and must have the ability to make decisions in order to affect one's outcome. With this in mind, I knew the students had to gain an awareness of their individual responsibility for each one's outcome before they could gain a consciousness and a kinesthetic or physical awareness of how to use their instruments consistently.

My consideration of Sartre's outlook on the individual being responsible for her outcome was instilled in the students. In making this principle explicit at the outset of the vocal instruction, a clear sense of awareness emerged for both the students and me. This was an important foundation to set for each student, because in order to be conscious of vocal development, as well as a stakeholder, she must be responsible. My goal was to help foster independence and autonomy in the students in the beginning of our work together, so as to build consistency and confidence leading to an exploration of freedom.

At the onset of the study and with varying depth, however, each student found the notion of being responsible and accountable in our student-teacher relationship a challenge for vocal development and learning consistency. My phenomenological reflection upon our relationship and the materials revealed the second theme to me: the theme was resistance.

Resistance

In some cases, it was apparent that the idea of being responsible was not a framework of instruction that had been experienced by the students prior to entering higher education. This may have contributed to the students' hesitance or resistance to be open to a new idea or approach. Both Katherine and Nina showed resistance to the idea of being a stakeholder in the process of learning vocal technique leading towards to independence. At the beginning of the study cycle, it appeared that Katherine and Nina were resistant to working towards making their own discoveries when guided by me and, instead, preferred to be led, to imitate how I sang a passage in a song or exercise, or to be told exactly how to do something sequentially. This preference may reflect an approach similar to those discussed in the scientific approaches and some contemporary approaches, in which there are scripted and sequential lessons and rote exercises. Both students showed a strong desire to find consistency in singing; however, early in the research study, they still wanted to be told how to do it "step by step," and perhaps were not gaining an awareness of what "felt right" or an awareness of the importance of facing responsibility at that point in the study (Katherine and Nina, Reflective Journals, 2013). Katherine wrote, "I find in my individual practice sessions I am having a difficult time warming up properly. I intend to bring this up in our next lesson" (Katherine, Reflective Journal, February 27, 2013). The idea that Katherine wrote "warming up" as opposed to considering the work done in a practice room as building technique and consistency showed resistance to taking responsibility and a lack of trust in a new idea or approach. She had not engaged in much vocal technique before entering university and exhibited reticence and a resistance to change when faced with the notion that she must learn independence in singing. Nina wrote, "I don't feel like I fully grasp how to sing the "correct" way. I truly believe I have a thin voice. I'm not sure what Susan sees that I don't!" (Nina, Reflective Journal, January 24, 2013). Nina, when asked in a reflective prompt to reflect, expressed a concern that we repeated some things in the lessons. "I do sometimes feel like we are doing the same things over and over again—but it is hard to tell if it is because I haven't learned something correctly or if we are just going through the motions" (Nina Reflective Journal, March 13, 2013). In this passage, Nina was resistant to two things. First, Nina displayed a lack of trust in the teaching approach that emphasizes the existentialist principles of responsibility and freedom. Second, and arguably more importantly, she was distrustful of herself in opening up to discovering her true sound. She had a negative outlook on her singing voice and resisted the teaching approach emphasising the notion of responsibility in her own singing. She was repeating the same technical problems over and over again in lessons, so it was necessary to revisit the same technical issues weekly. Her resistance to taking responsibility, and her lack of experimentation in finding her sound, resulted in her inability to find consistency in the practice room. By searching for rote exercises, she was unable to feel if what she was doing was the correct way to sing. When Nina merely attempted to imitate how I sang a passage in her lesson, she did not gain awareness of her own instrument. This was, arguably, a large obstacle to her finding her sound. Nina wished to follow a step-by-step formula to develop consistent singing, but in doing so, she was inhibiting her potential to find her own voice. To take responsibility for finding one's resonant tone takes patience and reflective practice, as well as experimentation.

This was a challenge for me to overcome in my student-teacher relationship. In order to consider a way to address this and help to guide Katherine and Nina though this resistance, I referred to Sartre's (1993) thoughts about the individual and her responsibility. Sartre (1993) wrote, "What happens to me happens through me, and I can neither affect myself with it nor revolt against it (p. 64). In this quote, Sartre is trying to address the notion of revolting against one's ultimate responsibility for one's outcome. He states that events will occur to one and through one, and that one cannot resist this occurrence. The initial reaction to awareness might be that of revolt. Sartre's (1993) term is "revolt against" what happens through oneself. This parallels the experiences that were described by the students in their resistance to taking on responsibility. I considered that the notion of being fully responsible was perhaps formidable for the students to accept and that their first reaction was to resist it. I was diligent, however, in facing my responsibility as the guide in this student-teacher relationship and continued working with Katherine and Nina, assuring them that they could trust the process—our process. I considered Sartre's (1993) account of the individual and the notion of being and responsibility. Sartre remarks, "Every event in the world can be revealed to me only as an opportunity" (p. 68). In considering this view, both in my own teaching approach and as I fostered the same notion in my students, I was able to present them with a different way to look at being responsible. I looked at the challenge of helping the students to feel comfortable with responsibility as an opportunity for me to be an effective instructor; one who could help my students mitigate inconsistency, resistance to responsibility, and other issues. I assured them that facing responsibility was a positive thing—an opportunity—and that in the long run they would be more independent and more technically proficient singers if they opened themselves up to making self-discoveries when guided by me, as opposed to merely attempting to imitate how I demonstrated a vocal passage or exercise in a lesson.

Katherine and Nina also resisted facing responsibility in Sartrean terms as the students were challenged to find consistency in their breath support. Their reaction was as before: to ask for scripted and sequential exercises. I continued to consider Sartre's (1993) notion that one must not resist responsibility and can instead view it as an opportunity. Instead of acquiescing to the students' resistance by giving scripted exercises for breath and a resonant tone, I worked with each student, using an individualised approach influenced by the existentialist principle of responsibility. In so doing, I guided them by using clear descriptions of the vocal anatomy, in which I explained how the respiratory system functions in relation to singing. I used diagrams and took a hands-on approach to show them on their bodies where exactly they should feel breath support. As well, I showed them diagrams of the resonating chambers in the head, so they had a visual representation of where they should feel the vibrations of their sound. I considered that this approach was much more effective and holistic in guiding them to discover their own breath and resonant tone.

As I continued to be fully aware of my responsibility as a facilitator of voice, I worked with Katherine and Nina by instructing each with an individualised approach. I worked diligently with the students to help them make the transition to find awareness of their instruments and the benefit of being responsible. As well, I worked to guide them to discover kinesthetic awareness, leading to consistency.

FEAR AND ANGUISH

While less prominent in one student, the theme of fear and anguish was presented through the students' written reflections of their experience. Sartre (2007) tells us that when one is faced with the realization of responsibility and freedom, one may experience varying states or feelings of anguish or abandonment. I considered this notion in my student-teacher relationships. It gave insight into some of the students' resistance to this approach at the early stages of the study and how they experienced their performances on stage. In the realization of responsibility and the ability to be free and to choose, one realises one is fully alone in one's choices and responsibility. This idea can cause fear and a state of anguish, in Sartrean terms. Katherine reflected on the notion of responsibility: "Responsibility can be daunting at times" (Katherine, Reflective Journal, April 12, 2013). Nina experienced fear in reaction to the notion of being responsible for her part in her vocal development, which she found intimidating. In reflecting on her earlier reaction to having to be responsible, Nina wrote that she experienced fear: "I do tend to find it scary" (Nina, Reflective Journal, April 13, 2013). Early in the study, these reflective posts showed a reaction of fear to the notion of being responsible for outcome.

When faced with responsibility, Nina and Katherine experienced feelings of anguish and abandonment, knowing they were fully responsible for themselves. The experience of fear and anguish occurred for Katherine and Nina in the practice room, and for Alexandra as well, although to a much lesser extent. Arguably, Nina and Katherine experienced anguish in the practice room because at the early stages of their work, they were resistant to embracing responsibility. Both Katherine and Nina searched for sequential, scripted exercises early in the study. These do not encourage individual awareness of one's instrument and merely serve to exercise the voice without focus. Because of this, they could not find much vocal consistency early in the study, and this caused them to experience anguish in their lack of vocal development and consistency. Nina wrote, "There is certainly disconnect in my sound from class to home practice" (Nina, Reflective Journal, January 5, 2013). At this point in the study, Nina was attempting to try sequential exercises at home and was not practicing to gain awareness of her tone; she did not trust our process at this point and wanted to continue singing as she did in choral rehearsals (in these rehearsals, the choir is often "warmed up" with scripted exercises). She was fearful of transitioning to the individualised experimentation with her vocal tone we did in her lessons in the practice room. She frequently faced the idea that she alone was ultimately responsible for determining her outcome and whether she gained consistency or not.

Nina experienced considerable anguish in her practice sessions at the early stages of the study, as she sought to imitate how she heard others sing instead of working to discover her own individual tone. Nina wrote, "It sounds like crap. Also, singing along with these videos solidifies how I feel about this. I can't create a sound like these soloists" (Nina, Reflective Journal, January 27, 2013). This passage suggests that Nina was suffering from both fear and anguish. In attempting to imitate singers she heard in video recordings of the songs she was studying she was not being responsible for herself. She was not working to discover her own sound; rather, she was letting fear and anguish in facing responsibility take over and, instead of working to discover her sound, she tried to imitate professional singers she heard in recordings.

The anguish and fear that Katherine faced early in the study in her practice sessions was related to a fear of facing responsibility in her vocal development and to a fear of sounding bad. She also attempted to imitate other singers in her past instead of working to find her own sound and working towards consistency. Katherine wrote, "I am having a difficult time with finding effective practice room methods" (Katherine, Reflective Journal, February 9, 2013). At this point in the study, Katherine was still struggling with the anguish of not finding consistency in her sound. She was still looking to accomplish this with a list of exercises instead of being responsible and working to discover her individual sound with me as the guide.

Unsurprisingly, this fear and anguish translated to the experience that Katherine and Nina had during performance. Though it may be a normal occurrence to have a certain amount of fear before performing, the experience that Nina and Katherine described during performance was, in fact, beyond this: they described it as panic. Katherine wrote, "After my performance this week, which didn't go amazingly, Susan and I discovered that perhaps my stage fright was becoming more of an issue than we had first believed" (Katherine, Reflective Journal, February 9, 2013). Nina also experienced a great deal of fear and anguish in a performance early in the study. She stated, "I was panicking. I lost my breath control it was totally embarrassing" (Nina, Reflective Journal, February 15, 2013).

I believe the anguish the students experienced and described was due in part to their insecurities about their proficiency as vocalists but, more importantly, it was due to their fear in taking responsibility for their vocal development. Sartre's (1993) idea of how one experiences anguish gives insight into how the students were possibly feeling. He wrote that the individual was "one who realizes in anguish his condition as being thrown into a responsibility" (p. 68). Sartre describes here a view of how one interprets the notion of responsibility. If one views responsibility as being thrown into something, then it is likely that anguish will occur. In the case of Nina and Katherine, it was apparent at this point in the study that they still viewed the concept of responsibility in a way that caused fear and anguish. They had been resistant to the idea of responsibility and were afraid of it. This translated to a lack of consistency and development, which heightened their experience of anguish in a performance situation. It was apparent that at this point in the study, when Katherine and Nina were alone on stage, that they experienced the feeling of being "thrown into" responsibility (p. 68). The moments that Katherine and Nina were on stage were an example of the realisation of which Sartre speaks, when one is alone and discovers one is solely responsible. The students came to the realisation that they were fully responsible, and they were in a state of anguish.

It is of interest to note that Alexandra did not experience fear and anguish in her practice sessions, nor in performance. She had an ability to transition from an acute awareness of her responsibility and ability to determine her outcome and essence to embracing the notion of finding freedom in singing and artistry. Alexandra wrote in response to a reflective prompt asking her about fear and anguish: "I have never had too much trouble with stage fright" (Alexandra Reflective Journal, March 2013). I believe she had a different, and perhaps more confident, view of herself than did the other students, and a different mindset from theirs. Accordingly, she did not experience feelings of fear and anguish in her practice sessions, nor in performance. She just experienced what many performers do prior to stepping out on the stage—a slight but manageable elevation in excitement. There was a notable difference in Alexandra's openness to Sartre's principles, as reflected in her journal and a great deal of openness during her sessions with me. She showed a clear willingness to take the risk to embrace responsibility from the outset of the study. This is the reason Alexandra does not appear frequently in the analysis of the theme of fear and anguish. As the relationship in the studio is one that is collaborative, and I am the guide, I am also influenced by Sartre's principles of fear and anguish. This notion did not cause anguish or fear in me as the facilitator, but rather it offered ways for me to reconsider and reposition how I instructed voice and promoted ways for me to consider being an effective guide.

It was apparent early in the study that Nina and Katherine were facing challenges in accepting and facing responsibility and freedom in our student-teacher relationship, and that this led to them to experience anguish and fear. I believe that improved vocal development through responsibility is the precursor to the ability to explore freedom and find emotional engagement in singing. It was necessary to reflect on my teaching approach to ensure that I was working with Katherine and Nina to help them move towards accepting responsibility, and that I was leading them towards an exploration of freedom. I considered the existentialist view of instruction in the classroom and how "Existentialism emphasizes the creation of ideas that are relevant to each student. This idea promotes viewing each student as an individual who is unique" (Segall and Wilson, 2004, p. 147). I reflected upon how I could continue to help Nina and Katherine make a connection or discovery in vocal development, and I considered how I was guiding the students.

I examined the way in which I was instructing the students to ensure I was offering them an individualised approach, considering them holistically (mind, body, spirit, emotions and experience) while fostering a humanistic student-teacher relationship. Drawing again from the broader existential framework in education, the principles inherent in humanistic instruction and student-teacher relationships explicitly emphasise one's care and concern, acting as a guide, responsibility, flexibility, instruction of the individual, and inspiration of both responsibility and freedom in students. I asked all three students in a reflective prompt later in the study to state if they felt they were instructed in an individualised, holistic and humanistic manner or not. Each student felt they were instructed both individually and holistically. Katherine wrote, "I feel like Susan catered to me in a personal manner" (Katherine, Reflective Journal, April 12, 2013). Alexandra's experience revealed the following comment, "Feedback is constantly changing depending on what the focus was in that particular lesson. If I came into a lesson claiming I was having trouble, further direction and tips for the issue would always be given" (Alexandra, Reflective Journal, April 12, 2013). Nina also experienced individualised instruction: "We absolutely address my specific technical needs as we work through pieces" (Nina, Reflective Journal, April 13, 2013). Each student also noted that she felt she was instructed holistically, in that I addressed them as a complete singer with body, mind, spirit, emotion, and experience considered in my approach. I worked to address each singer as an individual, instructing all aspects of what they needed to develop, drawing upon many of the varied approaches I reviewed in the earlier part of my study, and aware of my responsibility.

With this confirmation of individualised instruction from the students, I continued to teach each individual based upon Sartre's existentialist principles, working towards instilling responsibility and leading towards an exploration of freedom. Alexandra was already developing vocal consistency and working towards a deeper emotional connection. As the study continued, both Katherine and Nina eventually made significant changes in consistency, and their outlook on responsibility changed. The changes noted in Katherine and Nina as well as Alexandra's continued improvement illuminated the next theme of acceptance. This theme will be analysed in the next section of this study.

ACCEPTANCE

The student-teacher relationship I fostered in my voice studio guided Katherine, Nina and Alexandra to experience acceptance of responsibility. I drew upon Sartre's (1993) thoughts on a person's responsibility: "He must assume the situation with the proud consciousness of being the author of it" (p. 63). By considering this underpinning notion in my teaching framework, I was able to give the students a different view of having responsibility. I was able to help them accept the notion of being responsible, by fostering the idea that being responsible put them in charge and allowed them to be proud of their outcome. I believed this idea would help the students feel empowered when they accepted the notion.

The students' acceptance made it possible for each to find more consistency in singing. Finally accepting their responsibility and trusting the student-teacher relationship based in Sartre's principles opened them to the ability to find more focus and self-discovery in their practice sessions, and this led to more consistency in practicing. As well, acceptance of responsibility opened the students to discover more about themselves as singers, as they were not distracted by an inability to sing comfortably and could begin to emotionally connect to music and text.

Katherine experienced acceptance of her responsibility, and wrote, "I have learned so much about my personal responsibility as a singer from her" (Katherine, Reflective Journal, April 12, 2013). I was very conscious of Sartre's principles and persisted in our student-teacher relationship to help Katherine come to terms with and accept her responsibility, assuring her that this would lead to her being a more confident, technically proficient singer and, as Sartre (1993) implies, proudly conscious. Katherine indicated, "I have come to realize especially that taking on such responsibility almost always has a positive effect in the long run" (Katherine, Reflective Journal, April 12, 2013). This experience aligns with Sartre's (1993) views on responsibility and on being the author of one's situation. Katherine's acceptance and trust in me as facilitator helped her progress very quickly in her vocal development, as she was more focused and aware of her technical issues while practicing. She came to lessons with questions and participated more in our developmental and collaborative process together, rather than expecting an approach where I demonstrated how to sing something, and she attempted to imitate it. This rote/imitative style was how she had practiced in the past. We have different voices, so when Katherine attempted to imitate how I sang, her practicing habits did not lead to consistency or a discovery of her individual sound. She accepted her responsibility and trusted our student-teacher relationship at this point in the study. Katherine wrote: "We have crossed so many major technical flaws and have resulted in a great deal of success. I put a great deal of my trust in Susan and she has yet to fail me." She wrote further: "Susan has effectively broken down my technique and started from scratch (which is quite remarkable) and has started rebuilding my vocal technique" (Katherine, Reflective Journal, April 12, 2013). Katherine's acceptance of responsibility in our student-teacher relationship led her to start to find much more consistency and consciousness in her singing.

Nina also accepted her responsibility and thus found that she experienced a deeper connection to her instrument and how to use it better and more consistently. With her acceptance, she also experienced a more positive outlook and a sense of pride and empowerment. She was becoming more confident with the knowledge that she was responsible for and, as Sartre (1993) indicated, the "author" of her outcome. She wrote of her experience in a practice session:" I am finding a lot more breath control especially in my upper range and I am a lot more comfortable." She wrote further comments, such as "it felt really good, like I was grounded," and she noted after a practice session that several passersby walked in on her as she rehearsed in a public theatre and stated that, "the sound was magnificent!" (Nina, Reflective Journal, February 6. 2013). This acceptance was such a positive change for Nina, as she was often quite negative about her vocal ability during the research study. This gave a clear view into her experience, and a view of how acceptance of responsibility helped her in her outlook and vocal development. She was beginning to gain a much stronger kinesthetic (physical) awareness of her instrument and this was leading to a feeling of consistency. She wrote, "It's starting to feel like second nature" (Nina, Reflective Journal, February 17, 2013). Nina's acceptance was also beginning to help her alleviate the feelings of fear and anguish she had previously experienced in practicing, although perhaps she had not gained enough consistency to alleviate fear and anguish in performance just yet, as she noted in her performance comments several days before this journal post. This post does show however, that although she had a bad experience in the performance setting, she had clearly accepted responsibility in her vocal consistency, and she had moved on to continue her development. Her acceptance of responsibility led her to feel more in control of her own instrument and more confident in her own ability to perform: "I have found some ways to deal with this through this teaching approach. I have learned that muscle memory will take over in times of stress" (Nina, Reflective Journal, April 20, 2013). Sartre (2007) affirms that the notion of responsibility is a positive idea, "for no doctrine is more optimistic, since it declares that man's destiny lies within himself" (p. 40). This indicates that man is in control of his outcome, and that the idea of being in control of one's outcome is, in fact, an optimistic idea. This idea underpinned my teaching approach with each student and was particularly helpful in guiding Nina and Katherine towards accepting responsibility and feeling optimistic about the outcome.

Alexandra had perhaps the most natural progression in gaining awareness and accepting responsibility for her role in our student-teacher relationship. As I discussed earlier in this chapter, I believe each singer has a different view of themselves, and hence some had more self-confidence and were more open to the teaching approach than others at the beginning of the research study. I believe that Alexandra experienced the existentialist notion (2007) that one's destiny is in one's control in a positive way, based on her video materials and journaling. Alexandra experienced little to no resistance in facing her responsibility: "It was a slight challenge at first to take on so much, however I got used to it and my practice habits had majorly improved compared to before University" (Alexandra, Reflective Journal, April 12, 2013). She embraced the idea of reflective journaling and having performances video taped as a way to help some aspects of her acceptance of responsibility. Alexandra wrote:

> Doing the journal reflections and the videos was a really good reminder to keep up the practicing and to keep my repertoire in good shape. I really enjoyed doing the journal and I felt it made me think more about how and what I was practicing rather than wasting time in the practice room. (Alexandra, Reflective Journal, April 12, 2013)

It is important to note that the reflective journaling and knowledge that her performances were to be videotaped was not what fostered the existentialist notion of responsibility in Alexandra. This fostering of responsibility was guided by me as the instructor and facilitator. The journaling and videotaping were instrumental to Alexandra's acceptance of her responsibility; however, that it not to say that these were the only ways in which she found responsibility. Rather, they were indicative of the ways that Alexandra was able to find a heightened consciousness of how Sartre's principles informed her thinking about voice. Alexandra's acceptance of her responsibility early in the study quickly enabled her to experience a deeper connection to her instrument, with heightened consciousness and awareness. As well, Alexandra felt she gained the ability to begin to experience an emotional connection to her music.

In the analysis of this theme, I explored the students' experience of acceptance and its relation to responsibility, as well as my own as the guide in our student-teacher relationship. I discovered that as I guided the students with an existentialist framework leading them to accept responsibility, each of the students began to experience more consistency in performance and in practicing. This consistency led the students to begin to explore the possibilities of freedom, in terms of physical freedom in singing. Considering Sartre's (1984) ideas of freedom helped make the notion of accepting responsibility and finding freedom in the form of physical awareness and release of physical tension or holding much clearer. Sartre (1984), in discussing freedom, stated that "no limits to my freedom can be found except freedom itself, or if you prefer, that we are not free to cease being free" (p. 567). If one considers this idea in relation to a singer, there is a parallel. The singer who is physically free is a singer with a released vocal tone. Sartre (1984) wrote further, "he is wholly and forever free or he is not free at all" (p. 569). One may consider this idea in relation to a voice student who previously held tension in her body, or who did not sing with a released vocal tone or an awareness of how to do so, such as the students in this study. One who is not physically free as a singer cannot be wholly free in all aspects of freedom (artistically free and able define essence through free will). The students, prior to acceptance of responsibility, were not able to explore freedom in the sense of exploring or, more importantly, releasing themselves to an experience of physical freedom in singing.

Using Sartre's ideas of freedom to influence my teaching approach offered ways to facilitate a release of tension and heightened awareness in the students led them to a sense, or awareness, of physical freedom. Freedom in this aspect entailed a level of consistency in singing that enabled the students to find a release to the exploration of freedom both in body and mind. The experience of release helped the students discover how they could find freedom in other aspects. Upon releasing the body and mind to experience physical freedom, they found consistency, and this in turn opened the students to the notion of an ability to explore freedom in free will, artistic freedom, and freedom in determining essence. The other aspects of freedom will be considered further in the analysis of the next theme.

Nina was the quickest to gain an awareness of physical freedom in singing. She did not have too many physical tensions, and this made working on her breath support, release, and released resonant vocal tone a relatively seamless task. As the singer is the instrument, the mind, body, emotions, spirit, and experience must be free in order to find a fully released vocal tone. Nina wrote, "I don't tend to have any tension in my body when singing, I try to ensure that I remain relaxed, yet focused" (Nina, Reflective Journal, April 13, 2013). A deeper awareness of freedom in all aspects of singing will occur for Nina once she finds a deeper awareness of her ability to determine her outcome as a singer. In other words, once she embraces her freedom even more, she will discover that she has the power to alter her facticity as a singer. According to Sartre (2007), facticity is the sum of our facts about ourselves; some we can alter, and some we cannot. Nina has always viewed herself as a choral singer and felt safe and comfortable in a group setting. Here, she was challenging herself to alter her own facticity and working to deal with feelings of anguish and abandonment associated with this transition to total freedom.

Katherine had previously experienced some tension in her body when not accepting her responsibility to become aware of how to use her instrument well and consistently. She had too much movement in her body, which caused a lack of breath support and tension in her body, as well as a great deal of tongue and jaw tension, which translated to her sound being tense. If the body is tense, the vocal tone will be tense as singers are the instrument, and tension in the body translates to a tense sound (Bunch, 1997; Doscher, 1994). Katherine noted, "I was having many issues concerning jaw/tongue tension and short of breath in my vocal line" (Katherine, Reflective Journal, January 25, 2013). With an overarching framework of guiding Katherine towards freedom in the Sartrean sense, I worked with her, showing her diagrams of the anatomy that illustrated the tongue and the effect tongue and jaw tension can have on the vocal mechanism. As well, I showed her anatomical diagrams of the respiratory system to explain how the breath support functions in singing. This approach was based partially in science and anatomy. I also used a hands-on approach to help her find a release and freedom in the body to access more air, and I gave her strategies to release her tongue and jaw. This solution was also was based in a contemporary approach, as it used a meditative breath and attempted to create tension and then release in the body. This approach helped her find physical freedom, and she noted, "My tone was much more consistent this week" (Katherine, Reflective Journal, February 1, 2013). Instructing Katherine with an approach grounded in existentialist principles helped her gain a deeper awareness and experience of physical freedom in singing.

It is important to make clear that existentialist principles are not to replace existing approaches currently in practice, but rather that they offer a way to reconsider how one may use a number of approaches to address the individual needs of the student, such as I described in addressing Katherine's issues.

Alexandra's written reflections and video footage showed a release towards the notion of physical freedom in singing once she accepted her responsibility. Alexandra displayed physical tension in her shoulders. This affected freedom in her vocal tone, as she carried tension and restriction in her upper body. Alexandra also had a tendency to lock her knees. All this tension restricted her ability to take in a full breath as her body was not released, and this translated to tension in her vocal tone (Doscher, 1994). Alexandra expressed her difficulty in finding physical freedom: "Lately, I have been having trouble achieving a consistent, low grounded breath. When I breathe in the wrong place, I compensate by involving my shoulders" (Alexandra, Reflective Journal, February 5, 2013). Applying Sartre's (1984) notion that the person cannot be free unless wholly or completely free, I knew that it was important for Alexandra to find release or physical freedom in her body. If Alexandra was not able to find complete physical freedom, I knew it would be a challenge for her to be able to explore other aspects of freedom. I worked with Alexandra on being more focused on her body and on the release of tension using meditative techniques from the contemporary approaches that tense and then release the body. This helped her gain awareness and, consequently, more physical freedom in singing. Alexandra wrote of her experience: "I am noticing that I am able to engage my breath more and am more conscious of fully using and taking advantage of my breath while singing as opposed to getting the shoulders involved" (Alexandra, Reflective Journal, March 5, 2013). This realization by Alexandra showed a clear connection between accepting responsibility in vocal development leading to more consistent singing and an experience of physical freedom.

Acceptance of responsibility in vocal development and in our student-teacher relationship helped lead Alexandra and the other students to find physical freedom, and also led them to explore other aspects of freedom in singing; free will to determine essence and artistic freedom. The existentialist notion of freedom as free will and artistic freedom in expression was revealed to me through the students' materials and this uncovered the next theme, that of becoming.

BECOMING

The theme of becoming and its relation to Sartre's notion of freedom was revealed by what the students could envision for themselves upon acceptance of responsibility. In this section, I will discuss the idea of freedom as it relates to the students' free will in determining essence and artistic freedom and its parallel in what the students can become. Becoming is also an important theme for me as the researcher and vocal instructor. I discovered when determining my essence as the instructor. It might be similarly revealed to other instructors as they reconsider their student-teacher relationships.

The theme of becoming and its relationship to freedom is central in the application of Sartre's principles to vocal instruction, for it is the exploration of freedom that determines one's essence and outcome. The individual decides. Becoming aligns with the notion of essence according to Sartre (1984). Sartre says of essence, "I am not present to it in my actual presence but as about-to-become-myself" (p. 280). In this idea, Sartre speaks of the notion of the individual determining what she will become and the type of individual she will become; the individual is the author of her project or outcome. In Sartrean terms, it is about making choices and embracing free will to decide and determine one's outcome. When one looks at one's existence, one can determine what one will become in the future. For the voice students in this study, the theme of becoming revealed itself once the students accepted responsibility in our student-teacher relationship. When the students accepted their role in our relationship with me as the guide, they began to gain an ability to make connections, to be more aware of their instruments, and to find physical freedom in singing. Consistency led the students to gain insight into an experience of what they could become as singers. They could become independent, autonomous singers in a position or place to be able to emotionally connect to their music without the distraction of poor technical singing.

The video footage was the most valuable information to me in discovering the theme of becoming. Following the live performances, I was able to view whether there was a change in the emotional engagement in performance in the students or not. A change or deeper expression of emotions in performance from the students would arise as each student had the experience of individual exploration of freedom in both their free will to determine essence as well their choices in artistry. The theme of becoming arose from the students when they began to explore the notion of freedom upon acceptance of responsibility. As the instructor, the reflection with which I entered each student-teacher relationship made me more self-aware regarding my own exploration of my freedom and my effectiveness. An exploration into my free will revealed ways I could choose varied teaching approaches, making my choices in determining my essence and discovering ways to become a better instructor or facilitator rather than a "teacher" of voice. I had the opportunity to see what I could become as an instructor by making choices that helped me be more effective in my student-teacher relationships.

I begin, accordingly, with the theme of becoming as it relates to a deeper emotional connection in music for the students with a newfound consistency and the ability to define essence. Sartre (2007) explains that man exists "only after he defines himself" (p. 22). This idea aligns with the theme of becoming, as revealed through the experience of the students instructed in this teaching approach. The students were beginning to define themselves as singers and were becoming more complete in terms of consistency and emotional engagement. The videos of performances showed a much deeper consciousness and awareness of their instruments. This led the students to experience a sense of what they could become in terms of making emotional connections to their music and text.

Katherine found that in being instructed with this teaching approach she experienced what she was becoming in gaining vocal consistency and the ability to make discoveries. She was finding her own sound (vocal tonal quality), and she experienced a sense of becoming in her ability to define her essence as a singer: "I think with Susan's help, I have found my true sound. In the past, I would mimic other sounds I thought I was supposed to sound like" (Katherine, Reflective Journal, April 12, 2013). This reflective post gives us a clear view into Katherine's experience of becoming. She was discovering her authentic sound as a singer. This revealed itself to Katherine in her experience of physical freedom in singing leading to more consistency. Once accepting responsibility, she found more physical freedom and more consistency, leading to much more authenticity in her singing and the development of her true sound. This teaching approach gave her a glimpse of what she was becoming as a singer.

Katherine became very aware of her body and vocal tone and found improved consistency. She began to experience more of a sense of the singer she could become. Katherine presented an interesting challenge; specifically, she was an overly expressive but inauthentic performer. Katherine wrote, "I have always thought of myself as an expressive singer, but in the past this expressiveness was being channeled in the wrong fashion" (Katherine, Reflective Journal, April 12, 2013). For her, movement and perceived expressiveness were ways to distract from a lack of consistency and a great deal of insecurity. Katherine's way to express herself in the past was to move around extensively, because she thought that this was a feature of expressive singing. Katherine used this movement as a distraction for her audience, in order to cover up her technical inconsistencies. With responsibility in her vocal development, as well as a deeper kinesthetic awareness and ownership of her instrument, she became more authentically expressive and engaging to watch as a performer. Katherine became a different performer. She wrote:

> There has been a tremendous noticeable difference that has affected my entire approach to singing. It took a while for myself to figure it out, but I now sing technically well with expressiveness without moving around to cover up vocal flaws. (Katherine, Reflective Journal, April 12, 2013)

This reflection was a crucial discovery for Katherine in her ability to define herself. Katherine discovered that she could be a technically consistent singer, and so found a new outlook on singing; she became more expressive, with real emotions and artistry. Katherine wrote, "I am now able to sing expressively, with technical accuracies, vocal freedom and emotion. This has taken my performing to a new level" (Katherine, Reflective Journal, April 12, 2013). This reflective passage gives a strong sense that Katherine was starting to experience what she was becoming and could become. She became a more engaging singer to watch and, as an observer, I had a view into the true performer and artist, as did Katherine. I coined the term "glitter" as a prompt in lessons to remind her, if she was using distraction and "showy" movement, to be expressive instead of a real and authentic emotional connection to the music and text.

In existentialist terms, Katherine became able to determine her essence as a singer and performer. In so doing, she has created the opportunity to become what she wishes to become as a singer and performer. She knew she was not a consistent singer, although she thought she was expressive, prior to our work together in the study. In being instructed with this teaching approach, she discovered that she was not being truly expressive, and she decided that she wanted to become a more technically consistent and authentically expressive singer. In other words, she wanted to determine her essence. Once she faced the responsibility of being the one who must determine her ultimate outcome, she explored freedom and free will in making the choice to become a more expressive and consistent singer. She learned to make choices in performance that were unique to her and she could then sing in her relation/interaction to the music and text. She began exploring and finding artistic freedom and a strong sense of what she was becoming as a performer and musician. She learned to redefine her essence as a singer as well as her facticity as a singer. She was no longer limited to the perception that she could only consider herself a musical theatre performer without consistent technique. She could now consider herself a more technically consistent singer, who was capable of meeting the demands of operatic performances as well as continued performing in musical theatre.

Nina's video materials also showed a remarkable development in consistency and an ability to become more emotionally engaged. Early in the study cycle, we recorded a live performance in which she was completely overcome by nerves. She was unable to find her starting pitch in her song and sang the first part of the song completely out of tune and without any emotional engagement (Student Recital Video Footage, February 15, 2013). A consequent performance later in the study cycle showed a completely different singer (Nina, Performance Footage, April 16, 2013). Nina became much more aware of her instrument and sang with more consistency. She was also quite expressive. She had a much more positive experience in this performance and, although she still battled nerves and anxiety, the ability to sing with more consistency gave her more ownership of her instrument and allowed her to become emotionally engaged. Nina wrote of a performance: "I was shaking, but I just concentrated on my technique. I was nervous but it was ingrained in my muscle memory. I did really well!" (Nina, Reflective Journal, April 17, 2013). Nina continued to become more comfortable with being expressive. In this passage, Nina was reacting to her previous experience in dealing with nerves and showed that she was working towards a deeper emotional connection to her music.

Prior to this study, Nina was primarily a choral singer. She was not a music student, but a working professional, and was therefore not immersed in music studies each day as were the other student participants. Though her main focus in daily life was not vocal development, she did experience a drastic change in how she viewed her essence as a singer. This further shows the benefit of this teaching approach for a variety of students. She started to determine her essence and her outcome as a singer. I wanted to continue to help make her aware that she was "the author" of her situation, in this case, vocal study. I considered Sartre's (2007) account of an individual's freedom and free will in my student-teacher relationship with Nina. Sartre writes,

"...man is a free being who, under any circumstances, can only ever will his freedom, I have at the same time acknowledged that I must will the freedom of others" (p. 49). I was able to foster the ability to use free will in Nina. I had to use my free will as instructor and facilitator to discover and find ways to help Nina discover hers. With these notions of responsibility and freedom in mind, I continued to help Nina discover what she could become, to embrace her free will to make emotional choices in music, and to have more confidence in her approach to singing. As well, I felt it was my responsibility to help improve her overall self-confidence and to be proud of her accomplishments. As Nina noted, she had some issues of self-doubt. As she experienced an improvement in those doubts, Nina wrote, "We have dealt with these somewhat in lessons. The 'singing life lessons' as we call it." She continued, "So often, self-doubt takes a toll in performance, and talking about these types of issues are helpful in releasing any concerns" (Nina, Reflective Journal, April 13, 2013). Nina struggled for much of the study with awareness and resistance leading to fear about how to define her essence as a singer. She presumed that her facticity as singer meant that she was, and would remain, a choral singer. Her experience in this study was a powerful transformation and a strong sense of becoming. She discovered that she could choose to be a solo singer, and one who could strive to find more artistic freedom in singing. In so doing, she worked towards redefining her essence as a singer; she could continue to sing in the choral setting but sought out solo opportunities within her choral groups. Nina wrote, "I have found more freedom in artistic expression" (Nina, Reflective Journal, April 13, 2013). As well, she successfully auditioned for an *a cappella* classical singing group in which she was the only soprano. She was exploring freedom and free will to make choices that redefined her essence as a solo singer. She decided to undertake a Royal Conservatory Practical Voice exam, her first one, at an advanced level. This is an exam that many students take in preparation for or as part of higher education voice studies. The fact that she is a working professional and still wished to take an exam suggests that she was determining her own essence and how she defined herself as singer and performer. In addition, she was given an opportunity to be the soloist at a wedding. Prior to her participation in this study, such a task would have been overwhelming for her to face and would have caused her feelings of anguish. She decided to take this opportunity, and it led to other wedding performance invitations.

The review of the video materials for Alexandra showed that she experienced a sense of becoming early in the study. She was able to connect emotionally to her music very quickly. She developed considerable consistency in singing early in the study cycle, so I was able to move very quickly towards fostering a stronger emotional connection to music in Alexandra and a sense of being the author of her outcome, in Sartrean terms. I was able to give Alexandra tools to help her engage in the text and character of the songs she studied, and this led to a very complete singer, one with consistency in singing as well as a deep awareness of emotions. Alexandra wrote, "Performances are becoming more consistent because of improved technique and better understanding of the text" (Alexandra, Reflective Journal, January 22, 2013). This reflective post was written shortly after the study cycle began, and she was already becoming engaged emotionally. She wrote further, "After reading over the English translation a few more times I was feeling more emotionally involved" (Alexandra Reflective Journal, February 1, 2013). She was being responsible and making choices in freedom to find ways to become more emotionally engaged as a singer.

Very quickly, Alexandra embraced the notion of being responsible for her instrument and for the development of vocal technique in our student-teacher relationship. With this vocal facility established early in the research study, Alexandra was able to explore free will and make choices in exploring her artistic freedom to see the possibilities of what she could become. She experienced a change in her emotional connection to her songs with a newfound consistency in singing. As her vocal consistency improved, Alexandra had the experience of being able to focus more on the emotions of a piece when singing. Alexandra wrote of her freedom to choose, "Although I am in the early stages of my degree, I felt like I was given the proper guidance and tools and that I get to decide what to do with them" (Alexandra, Reflective Journal, April 12, 2013). This reflective passage showed a strong sense of what she was becoming as a singer and performer. Alexandra grasped Sartre's (2007) notion that she was the author of her outcome. She wanted to work quickly to find consistency in singing to be able to explore and experience a deeper emotional connection in her music, as well as to become a more artistic performer. When Alexandra approached learning new songs, she had more ease in making discoveries in how to experience the song comfortably and how to memorise the feeling in her muscle memory with vocal consistency. As she prepared new repertoire, she was also able to find a strong emotional connection to the piece as she was learning it. She became able to define and do what she wanted to do in performance through exploring her artistic freedom and could see what she could become as a singer. As she worked through songs or arias in other languages (Italian and French, for example), she found a strong emotional connection to the text and character after translating the pieces and speaking the text, imagining the scene that was being described in the lyrics. I gave her some ideas as to how to find ways to connect emotionally to music and to reflect on the emotions she felt while speaking the text, so that she could bring those to the song in performance and use these ideas to make choices in artistic freedom.

Alexandra was able to become very engaged in her performances and make choices or decisions about how she would interpret a song in her own way. Alexandra wrote, "I am finding the tip of going through the pieces as a monologue very helpful. Taking out the notes and figuring out what each phrase means to me really helps sing the piece expressively" (Alexandra, Reflective Journal, March 6, 2013). These tools gave her a way to explore freedom and free will in choices of interpretation. In this passage, Alexandra experienced her songs at a deep emotional level. She was using her free will to make unique decisions about how she would like to emotionally connect to each of her pieces. Alexandra was very excited by the possibilities of what she could become and embraced exploring freedom and being the one who ultimately decided what she would become and her essence as a singer. Alexandra wrote, "Once different technical issues are not a problem, it becomes much easier to focus on the music and making it a great performance" (Alexandra, Reflective Journal, April 12, 2013). As well, she was finding ways to explore freedom to define her essence as a singer and performer and alter her facticity. She made the decision to be a consistent singer, and one that was expressive and emotionally connected to music. One of the ways that Alexandra found freedom to alter her facticity was to decide that, although she is not required to give a graduation recital for her particular voice major in music, she will audition for the music faculty to give a solo recital before she graduates. Alexandra embraced the notion of freedom and the aspects of free will, choices in artistic freedom and in determining her own essence as a singer. She gained a strong sense of self in being instructed with this teaching approach based in existentialist principles.

As an instructor, I came to my awareness of freedom as I discovered how important it is to consider Sartre's notion of freedom and the free will to choose from a number of approaches to help each student find consistency and to lead them to emotional engagement. This notion was tied to responsibility, as each principle is interconnected. However, my awareness of my freedom and ability to choose was crucial in the student-teacher relationships and influenced my effectiveness.

As I interpreted the themes that emerged, I realised that many of them also applied to me as instructor and facilitator. I interpreted my role of responsibility in the student-teacher relationship; I discovered that, as an instructor, facing one's responsibility is crucial. I became very aware of my responsibility. I accepted this responsibility without resistance, fear, or anguish. I experienced a sense of becoming, had a stronger awareness of my ability to facilitate individuated vocal instruction, and was able to reposition my essence as a voice instructor.

I considered van Manen's (1990) view of pedagogy, as in "what does it mean to 'listen' to pedagogy?" (p. 149). What it meant to me as the voice instructor in this research study was that it was necessary for me to "listen" in all aspects. I was to view each student with a heightened consciousness and awareness such as Sartre (1984) described, and I was to listen to and interpret the materials of the students' experience. In listening to pedagogy in this study, I was attentive to the needs of each student and was flexible in how I approached their varied needs. In listening to the pedagogy, I found a deeper meaning in how I instructed the students, and a better understanding of my essence as an instructor and facilitator. I strove to ensure that I was the guide to their discoveries. If a student indicated she was not making a physical or kinesthetic connection to something we worked on in lessons, I used a different approach to explain it to her to ensure consistency in singing.

Voice instructors are the guides who strive to be effective vocal instructors. Inherent in this role/expectation, there is an implicit understanding that instructors listen to students' needs and be adaptive to them. This approach calls forth and instills a sense of responsibility in the process of vocal development in our students; moreover, it also requires the instructor to be responsible and to guide the students to their discoveries as individuals. Drawing upon these principles made me attentive to the increasing importance and obligation that my role entailed in the student-teacher relationship. In consideration of an approach influenced by Sartre, it was important for me to ask the students whether they believed I faced my responsibility in instructing each of them. Each student thought that I did. Katherine stated, "I think Susan went above and beyond her responsibility she genuinely cared about my progress, and had the perfect balance of strictness and gratification when it came to my improvements and goals" (Katherine, Reflective Journal, April 12, 2013). Alexandra experienced this teaching approach as "Always engaged and wanting us to do our best. As a vocal teacher, you were strict enough when you needed to be however always encouraging" (Alexandra, Reflective Journal, April 12, 2013). Nina's thoughts on the notion of responsibility in this teaching approach were reflected in her comment, "You are very engaged in the process of my vocal development, constantly showing me what I was doing incorrectly, and also providing positive support when something was done right" (Nina, Reflective Journal, April 13, 2013).

The notion of responsibility and how it influenced my teaching approach were very much based in a humanistic approach. I consider these to be effective strategies for an instructor, ones that align with existentialist principles closely. They are arguably part of the equation in how instructors are to reposition their teaching practices regarding the student-teacher relationship in the vocal studio.

In grounding the teaching approach drawing upon existentialist thought and the influence of Sartre's views on the principles of responsibility and freedom, I was able to determine my essence as instructor. I wished to become a more effective instructor for my voice students, and so I made choices to determine my outcome and my essence as an effective facilitator of vocal instruction in higher education.

Conclusion

Upon reviewing reflective and video information from the students lived experience, as well as my own experience in this study, I was able to draw some conclusions based on my research question:

> To what extent can Jean-Paul Sartre's existentialist principles of responsibility and freedom suitably influence the student-teacher relationship and be applied to vocal development to improve inconsistent and emotionally unengaged singing in undergraduate music students?

The revelation and interpretation of the themes that emerged may offer ways for a vocal instructor to consider ways to become more effective. She may wish to attempt to create a humanistic teaching environment with an existentialist framework that complements how she already instructs. I believe that an instructor who faces her responsibility, one who instills it in her students, and who strives to find her own freedom as well as guiding students to theirs, may mitigate inconsistency and lack of engagement in today's voice students.

When instructed with this teaching approach influenced by Sartre's principles, the students faced responsibility and found improved consistency in singing. They emerged more independent and autonomous. Each student experienced this consistency at various depths, and each found improved development. As well, each student noted the discovery of aspects of individual freedom. Aspects of freedom that emerged from this study were an awareness of physical freedom in singing and a way to release the body and mind. Each student also experienced a profound change in artistic freedom and an awareness of her ability to determine her essence through free will and choice. As each student embraced responsibility, she found more consistency, as Sartre's principles influenced the teaching approach. With this consistency, the students were able to find meaning in their music. They improved their ability to explore emotions and to find ways to make personal interpretations through considering freedom in artistry in their music; thus, each created an aesthetic experience in performance for both the student and her audience.

I believe this teaching approach influenced by Sartre's principles may create ways to reposition how instructors view their role in their student-teacher relationships in the voice studio and may complement approaches they are already using. As well, it may be considered for use in helping a voice instructor foster better and more consistent singing and emotional engagement in her students. This study presented ways to show instructors how to approach the facilitation of voice and offered a view of both the student's and the instructor's phenomenological experience in using this approach. This occurred through considering each student in existentialist terms as a blank slate and as an individual, by offering instruction based on the exploration of responsibility and freedom, and by addressing the student's specific needs to help improve consistency. This instruction was facilitated in a humanistic manner in which I, while being responsible, explored freedom to draw upon numerous teaching approaches described in the review of pedagogical approaches in this study. I believe this approach based in existentialist thought was holistic, in that it addressed all aspects of the student, the body, mind, spirit, and experience It was, as well, a holistic approach for me as the instructor, given that I was conscious of the same aspects.

As I taught the students, I effectively addressed the body using varied approaches that led to improved consistency in singing. I instructed the mind, both by instilling responsibility and in developing the consciousness and awareness of how to sing correctly with consistency. I guided them to open their minds to freedom and to explore how freedom informed their singing, thus enhancing their experience in singing. I believe that the possibilities of exploration of freedom and what they can become in artistic interpretations can be endless for a singer using this approach. With freedom and consistency in singing, the student can experience a new interpretation of a song each time she sings it. She is completely free to determine her own essence and what she can become. As well, the study served to give instructors consideration of what they can become, and to reflect upon ways to be more effective in their student-teacher relationships in higher education. I consider that "pedagogy is something that a parent or teacher continuously must redeem, retrieve, regain, recapture in the sense of recalling" (van Manen, 1990, p. 149). It is important that vocal pedagogues continue to strive to facilitate voice students in a way that fosters artistry. This can be accomplished through self-reflection, by recapturing ways to address the complete singer to foster artistic performances, and through a continued passion for the performing arts in higher education voice students.

CHAPTER 6

Unlocking the Potential of Singers

FINAL CONCLUSIONS

This research study aimed to provide the foundation for a view of the student-teacher relationship based in a theoretical framework influenced by the existentialist principles of Jean-Paul Sartre. The teaching approach considered in this study was not a prescribed method for vocal instructors, but rather offered an approach or way to reconsider or reposition the student-teacher relationship in the voice studio and a deeper awareness of being. The approach emphasized both an acceptance of responsibility and a respect for and exploration of freedom in the student-teacher relationship in the voice studio. It highlighted the importance of both responsibility and freedom in teacher and student relationships. For the student taught with this approach, there is a reclaiming of the body, simply beyond vocal technique. It is attending to the notion of gaining agency and empowerment. To explore what it means to be a singer and artist. It is not simply just about regulating the body through consistency, but raising a level of consciousness about what it means to be a singing artist and the possibilies this presents.

I discovered the notion of responsibility presented a challenge for some of the students in this study. Sartre's (2007) idea that one is ultimately responsible for one's outcome elicited a reaction or experience of resistance with feelings of fear and anguish for some students. The acceptance of this responsibility, however, ultimately gave the singers the opportunity to unlock their fears and inhibitions about singing by finding their own sound as individuals. In so doing, it gave them permission to go beyond their comfort level, and step into the role of singers with a different view of what it means to be human.

The influence of the principles guided my own exploration of responsibility and freedom and my free will, and gave me the opportunity not to be locked into using just one approach, as that might not have addressed the individual needs of the students in this study. This realization gave me ways to become more effective for the students, and it influenced the way I interacted with the students. As well, the influence of Sartre's ideas on freedom to determine essence also gave me a way to reflect upon myself as the facilitator in this relationship. It gave me a means to view myself through an existentialist lens, to see that I could, in fact, determine my essence as an instructor of voice. This ability to define the effectiveness of my instruction through the influence of existentialism was of great benefit to the students, as I was to decide what type of facilitator I wished to be.

Sartre's notion of freedom influenced the students in this relationship. Once they were able to accept responsibility in our student-teacher relationship, they were more open to the possibilities of what they could become as singers. They were given a way to view themselves as consistent and emotionally engaged artists and were empowered to take steps on the path to becoming that type of singer and performer. They also experienced freedom in the experience of discovering the endless possibilities of interpretation in music and text. There was no prescribed way to interpret a song or text; they were exposed to the freedom to decide how to be unique and individual in their performances. An exploration of freedom gave the students a view of what they could become as singers and released them to experiment and to take risks in performance by exploring individual interpretations of their music and texts. Existentialist thinking gave me the opportunity to gain a deeper awareness of myself as a teacher and human interacting with another human. It helped to slow everything down to a pace where there was more time to listen; to process thus allowing me to be more effective for my students.

Existentialism examines the human condition and humanity. By giving singers and teachers the opportunity to look at themselves through a different - and perhaps more fine-tuned lens, it offers the chance for one to unearth a deeper awareness of oneself as an artist. It can give a deeper appreciation for what it is to be a vessel through which the works of composers and music are channeled - making an even more lasting impact on humanity as an artist. One simply has to take stock of the void that has been left in world from the inability to perform to live audiences – or with one another given the current pandemic (2020) to gain an understanding of just how important the experience of music is to mankind. As we make our way as a civilization out of this void – and once again experience live music, it is my hope that this study may inspire singers and teachers to reflect on how vital their art is, and what is means to be a singer and teaching artist.

REFERENCES

Acadia University (2020). School of Music. Retrieved from http://music.acadiau.ca/

Alchemy of Singing (2020). Retrieved from http://www.aosinging.com/home.html

Alderson, R. (1979). *Complete handbook of voice training.* West Nyack, NY: Parker Publishing.

Alexander, F. M. (2001). *The use of the self.* London: Orion Publishing. (Original work published 1932).

Appelman, D. R. (1974). *The science of vocal pedagogy.* Bloomington: Indiana University Press. (Original work published 1967).

Barnes, H. (1973). *Sartre.* New York: Lippincott.

Barnes-Burrow, K., Lan, W., Edwards, E., & Archambeault, N. (2008). Current attitudes toward voice studio teaching technology: A bicoastal survey of classical signing pedagogues. *Journal of Voice, 22*(5), 590-602.

Barritt, L., Beekman, T., Bleeker, H., & Mulderij, K. (1984). Analyzing phenomenological descriptions. *Phenomenology + Pedagogy, 2*(1), 1-17.

Bauer, J. M. (1983). *An introduction to the philosophical and psychological foundations of teaching choral conducting and organ.* Retrieved from ProQuest Digital Dissertations. (UMI 8798122)

Baylor University (2020). School of Music. Retrieved from http://www.baylor.edu/music/

Berklee College of Music (2020). Retrieved from http://www.berklee.edu/

Bernac, P. (1970). *The interpretation of French song.* New York: W. W. Norton.

Blades-Zeller, E. (2003). *A spectrum of voices: Prominent American voice teachers discuss the teaching of singing.* Lanham, MD: Scarecrow Press.

Bowen, G. (2009). Document analysis as a qualitative research method. *Qualitative Research Journal, 9*(2), 27-40.

Bowers, C. (1965). Existentialism and education theory. *Educational Theory, 15*(3), 222-229.

Brennan, R., (2004). *The Alexander Technique manual: Take control of your life and posture.* London: Connections Book Publishing.

Brighouse, H., & Swift, A. (2006). Equality, priority, and positional goods. *Ethics 116* (3), 471-497.

Broudy, H. S. (1971). Sartre's existentialism and education. *Educational Theory, 21*(2), 155–177.

Brown, C. A. (2000). *A humane approach to private piano instruction: An analysis and application of the ideas of Abraham Maslow, Carl Rogers, and Jerome Bruner.* Retrieved from ProQuest Digital Dissertations. (UMI 3045990)

Brunk, A. (2008). The private studio: Managing voice problems in the private studio. *Journal of Singing, 64*(5), 615-618.

Bruser, M. (2011). Making music. In B. Boyce & the Shambhala Sun (Eds.), *The mindfulness Revolution: Leading psychologists, scientists, artists, and meditation teachers on the power of mindfulness in daily life* (106-112). Boston: Shambhala Publications.

Bunch, M. (1997). *Dynamics of the singing voice.* Vienna; New York: Springer-Verlag.

Bunch Dayme, M. (2005). *The performer's voice: Realizing your vocal potential.* New York: W.W. Norton.

Bunch Dayme, M. (2006). An argument for whole body and holistic approaches to research in singing. *Journal of Singing, 63* (1), 59-64.

Burger, J. (2011). *Personality.* (8th ed.). Belmont, CA: Wadsworth.

Burstow, B. (1983). Sartre: A possible foundation for educational theory. *Journal of Philosophy of Education, 17*(2), 171-185.

Caccini, G. (2009). *Le nuove musiche* (2nd ed.) H. W. Hitchcock (Ed.). Middleton, WI: A-R Editions. (Original work published 1601).

Calhoun, R. J. (1963). Existentialism, phenomenology, and literary theory. *South Atlantic Bulletin, 28*(4), 4-8. jg8d

Callaghan, J. (2000). *Singing and voice science.* San Diego, CA: Singular Publishing Group.

Callaghan, J., & Wilson, P. (2004). *How to see and sing: Singing pedagogy in the digital era.* Surry Hills, NSW: Cantare Systems.

Camden County College (2020). Retrieved from http://www.camdencc.edu/

Caruso, E., & Tetrazzini, L. (1975). *Caruso and Tetrazzini on the art of singing.* New York and London: Dover Publications. (Original work published 1909).

Clements, J. F. (2008). *The use of imagery in teaching voice to the twenty-first century student.* Retrieved from ProQuest Digital Dissertations. (UMI 3321469)

Cleveland, T. (1994). A clearer picture of singing voice production: 25 years of progress. *Journal of Voice, 8*(1), 18-23.

Cobb-Jordan, A. (2001). The study of English, French, German and Italian techniques of singing related to the female adolescent voice. Retrieved from ProQuest Digital Dissertations. (UMI Number 1409833)

Cole, A. (2011). Choosing the best approach for vocal pedagogy. Retrieved from
   http://www.acole.net/downloadable_works-65.html

Colton, R. K, & Estill, J. (1981). Elements of voice quality: Perceptual, acoustic and physiologic aspects. In N. J. Lass (Ed.), *Volume V, Speech and language: Advances in basic research and practice*. New York: Academic Press.

Creswell, J. (1994). *Research design: Qualitative and quantitative approaches*. Thousand Oaks, CA: Sage Publications.

Creswell, J. (2006). *Qualitative inquiry and research design: Choosing among five approaches* (2nd ed.). Thousand Oaks, CA: Sage Publications.

Dalhousie University (2020). Department of Music. Retrieved from
   http://www.dal.ca/faculty/arts/school-of-performing-arts/music.html

David, M. (1995). *The new voice pedagogy* (2nd ed.). Lanham, MD: Scarecrow Press.

Deere, J. D. (2002). Surveying and relating approaches and styles in the pedagogy of singing among voice teachers in six southeastern states. Retrieved from ProQuest Digital Dissertations. (UMI 3049155)

Deere, J. D. (2005). *Singing in the 20th century: A recollection of performance & pedagogy*. Bloomington, IN: AuthorHouse.

Degenhardt, M. A. B., (1975). Sartre, Imagination and Education. Journal of Philosophy of Education, 9(1), 72-92.

Denver Center for Performing Arts (2013). Retrieved from
   http://www.denvercenter.org/home.aspx

Deva, J. (1994). *The contemporary vocalist improvement course*. Sunland, CA: Jeannie Deva Enterprises.

Dhawan, M. L. (2005). *Philosophy of education*. Delhi: Isha Books.

Doscher, B. (1994). *The functional unity of the singing voice*. Lanham, MD: Scarecrow Press.

Dublin Institute of Technology (2020). Retrieved from http://www.dit.ie/conservatory/

Dufault, J. E. (2008). Three exemplary voice teachers: David Adams, Stephen King, & Patricia Misslin; Their philosophies & studio techniques. Retrieved from ProQuest Digital Dissertations. (UMI 3328303)

Earnshaw, S. (2006). *Existentialism: A guide for the perplexed*. London: Continuum International Publishing Group.

Eastman School of Music (2020). Retrieved from http://www.esm.rochester.edu/

Eberle, K. (2003). Enhancing voice teaching with technology. *Journal of Singing, 59*(3), 241-246.

Edwin, R. (2011). Pedagogic pears: Exploring vocal resonance. *Journal of Singing, 68*(2), 193-194.

Eisner, E. (1976). Educational connoisseurship and criticism: Their form and function in educational evaluation. *Journal of Aesthetic Education, 10*(3), 135-150.

Eisner, E. (1985). *The art of educational evaluation: a personal view*. Philadelphia, PA: Falmer Press.

Eisner, E. (2002). *The arts and the creation of the mind*. New Haven, CT: Yale University Press.

Elias, J., & Merriam, S. (2005). *Philosophical foundations of adult education*. Malabar, FL: Krieger.

Elliott, D. (1995). *Music matters*. New York: Oxford University Press.

Elliott, M. (2007). *Singing in style: A guide to vocal performance practices*. New Haven, CT: Yale University Press.

Elliot, M, (2010). Singing and mindfulness. *Journal of Singing, 67*(1), 35-40.

Epps, J., Smith, J. R., & Wolfe, J. (1997). A novel instrument to measure acoustic resonances of the vocal tract during phonation. *Measurement Science and Technology, 8*(10), 1112–1121.

Estill Voice Training™ (2020). Retrieved from http://www.estillvoice.com/pages/about-estill-voice

Feldenkrais, M. (1990). *Awareness through movement: health exercises for personal growth*. London: Arkana. (Original work published 1972).

Feldenkrais, M. (2002). *The potent self: a study of spontaneity and compulsion*. Berkeley, CA: North Atlantic Books. (Original work published 1985).

Feldman, A. (2002). Existential approaches to action research. *Educational Action Researcher, 10*(2), 233-251.

Feldman, A. (2009). Existentialism and action research. In S. Noffke and B. Somekh (Eds.), *The Sage handbook of educational action research* (381-391). Thousand Oaks, CA: Sage Publications.

Fields, V. A. (1947). *Training the singing voice. An analysis of the working concepts contained in recent contributions to vocal pedagogy*. Morningside Heights, NY: King's Crown Press.

Fields, V. A. (1970). Review of the literature on vocal registers. *NATS Bulletin, 26*, 6-7.

Findlay, L. (2009). Debating phenomenological research methods. *Phenomenology and Practice, 3*(1), 6-25.

Flick, U. (2009). *An introduction to qualitative research* (4th ed.). London: Sage Publications.

Flynn, T. (2006). *Existentialism: A very short introduction*. Oxford: Oxford University Press.

Folsom, R. L. (2011). The undergraduate pedagogy experience: Communication through academic freedom. *Journal of Singing, 67*(4), 403-407.

Foster, D. L. (1971). Existentialism and music education. *Music Journal, 29* (7), 39, 77.

Frederick, T. (2006). Hoarseness: The top causes and how to avoid it. *Canadian Musician, 28*(5), p. 32.

Gadamer, H. G. (1977). *Philosophical hermeneutics*. (D. E. Linge, Trans. & Ed.). Berkeley, CA: University of California Press. (Original work in *Truth and Method* published 1960).

Glaros, P. (2006). Technology in the private studio: A never ending story. *Journal of Singing, 62*(5), 567-572.

Gray, S. (2000). Cellular physiology of the vocal folds. *Otolaryngologic Clinics of North America, 33*(4), 679-697.

Greene, M. (1973). *Teacher as stranger*. Belmont: Wadsworth.

Greene, M. (1978). Teaching: The question of personal reality. *Teachers College Record, 80*(1), 23-35.

Greene, M. (1983). How I came to phenomenology. *Phenomenology + Pedagogy, 1*(1), 3-4.

Greene, M. (1991). Aesthetic literacy. In R. Smith & A. Simpson (Eds.), *Aesthetics and arts education* (149-161). Chicago: University of Illinois Press.

Greene, M. (1995). *Releasing the imagination. Essays on education, the arts, and social change*. San Francisco: Jossey-Bass.

Gregg, J. W. (2001). Resonation and articulation a new concept. *Journal of Singing, 58*(2), 167-169.

Greschner, D. (2007). Review of the naked voice: A wholistic approach to singing. *Journal of Singing, 64*(2), 239-242.

Groenewald, T. (2004). A phenomenological research design illustrated. *International Journal of Qualitative Methods, 3*(1), 42-55.

Guildhall School of Music and Drama (2020). Retrieved from http://www.gsmd.ac.uk/

Harer, J., & Munden, S. (2009). *The Alexander Technique resource book: A reference guide*. Lanham, MD: Scarecrow Press.

Harper, R. (1955). Significance of existence and recognition for education. In N. Henry (Ed.), *Modern philosophies and education* (215-258). Chicago: University of Illinois Press.

Hatch, J. A. (2002). *Doing qualitative research in educational settings*. Albany, NY: SUNY Press.

Heath, C., Hindmarsh, J., & Luff, P. (2010). *Video in qualitative research: Analysing social interaction in everyday life*. London: Sage Publications.

Helding, L. (2012). Mindful voice: Science and art and true grit. *Journal of Singing, 69*(1), 67-73.

Herr, K, & Anderson, G. (2005). *The action research dissertation: A guide for students and faculty*. Thousand Oaks, CA: Sage Publications.

Hines, J. (1982). *Great singers on great singing*. New York: Doubleday.

Holland, R. J. (2008). *National schools of singing and their impact on teaching vocal pedagogy and literature*. 17th Annual Convention of the Global Awareness Society International, May 2008, San Francisco, CA.

Honda, K, Hirai, H, Estill, J., & Takhura, Y (1994). Contribution of vocal tract shape to voice quality: MRI data and articulatory modeling. In O. Fujimura and M. Hirano (Eds.), *Vocal fold physiology: voice quality control*. San Diego: Singular Publishing.

Hycner, R. (1985). Some guidelines for the phenomenological analysis of interview data. *Human Studies, 8*(3), 279-303.

Indiana University (2020). Department of music. Retrieved from http://music.indiana.edu/

International Feldenkrais Federation (2020). Retrieved from http://feldenkrais-method.org/en

International Voice Teachers of Mix (2020). Retrieved from http://www.ivtom.org/

Jaspers, K. (1970). *Philosophy 2*. (E. B. Ashton, Trans.). Chicago: University of Chicago Press.

Joliveau, E., Smith, J., & Wolfec, J. (2004). Vocal tract resonance in singing: The soprano voice. *Journal of the Acoustical Society of America, 116*(4), 2434-2439.

Jones, F. P. (1997). *Freedom to change: The development and science of the Alexander Technique*. London: Mouritz.

Kansas University (2020). Vocal Pedagogy. Retrieved from http://web.ku.edu/~cmed/chovoped/chovopeddoc.html

Kirkpatrick, A., & McLester, J. R. (2012). Teaching lower laryngeal position with EMG biofeedback. *Journal of Singing, 68*(3), 253-260.

Kmucha, S., Yanagisawa, E., & Estill, J. (1990). Endolaryngeal changes during high-intensity phonation videolaryngoscopic observations. *Journal of Voice, 4*(4), 346-354.

Kneller, G. F. (1958). *Existentialism and education*. New York: Philosophical Library.

Lamperti, F. (1980). *The art of singing*. (J. C. Griffith Rev. and Trans.). New York: Schirmer. (Original work published 1890).

Lamperti, G.B., (2009). *G. B. Lamperti: The technics of bel canto.* G. Blankenbehler, (Ed.). United States: Pitch Perfect Publishing Company. (Original work published 1905).

Laverty, S. M. (2003). Hermeneutic phenomenology and phenomenology: A comparison of historical and methodological considerations. *International Journal of Qualitative Methods, 2*(3), 21-35.

Lehmann, L. (1993). *How to sing.* Mineola, NY: Dover Publications. (Original work published 1924).

Lieberman, C. (1985). The existentialist "school" of thought: Existentialism and education. *The Clearing House, 58*(7), 322-326.

Linsenbard, G. (2010). *Starting with Sartre.* London: Continuum International.

LoVetri, J. (2008). Contemporary commercial music. *Journal of Voice, 22*(3), 260-262.

Lyu, K. (2020). Holistic Voice Instructor. Retrieved from http://www.holisticvoicecoach.com/

Maharishi School of Management (2020). Department of Music http://www.mum.edu/music

Mahmud, J. (2009) *Psychology: Systems and theories.* New Delhi: APH Publishing.

Manchester School of Music (2020). Retrieved from http://www.manchesteracademy.net/

Manhattan School of Music (2020). Vocal Pedagogy. Retrieved from http://www.msmnyc.edu/Instruction-Faculty/Outreach

Manifold, L. (2008) Vocal pedagogy: How the application of breath and body management techniques improves the sound of singers. Retrieved from http://www.manifoldmelodies.com/docs/Manifold_breathing.pdf

Mannes College of Music (2020). Retrieved from http://www.newschool.edu/mannes/

Marchesi, M. (1970). *Bel canto: A theoretical and practical vocal method.* New York: Dover. (Original work published 1898).

Marino, G. (2004). *Basic writings in existentialism.* New York: Modern Library.

Mars Hill College (2020). Department of Music. Retrieved from http://www.mhc.edu/music

Martin D., & Loomis, K. (2007). *Building teachers: A constructivist approach to introducing education.* Belmont CA: Thomson Wadsworth.

Martyna, W. (1978). What does 'he' mean? Use of the generic masculine. *Journal of Communication, 28*(1), 131-138.

Martyna, W. (1980). Beyond the he/man approach: The case for non-sexist language. *Signs: Journal of Women in Culture and Society, 5*(3), 482-493.

Mastrangeli, I. (2020). Holistic Voice Lessons. Retrieved from http://www.erenemusic.com/lessons.html

Mathis, D. (2009). *Melodic sculpting: The art and science of singing.* Bloomington, IN: AuthorHouse.

McGill University (2020). Vocal Pedagogy. Retrieved from http://www.mcgill.ca/study/2011-2012/faculties/music/graduate/programs/master-music-mmus-performance-vocal-pedagogy-thesis

McKinney, J. (1994). *The diagnosis and correction of vocal faults: A manual for teachers of singing and for choir directors.* Long Grove, IL: Waveland Press.

McPherson, G. (Ed.). (2002). *The science and psychology of music performance.* New York: Oxford University Press.

Merleau-Ponty, M. (1962). *Phenomenology of perception.* (Routledge & K. Paul, Trans.). London: Routledge & Kegan Paul. (Original work published in French, 1945).

Merleau-Ponty, M. (1969). *The visible and the invisible.* (Northwestern & A. Lingis, Trans.). Evanston, IL: Northwestern Press & Alphonso Lingis. (Original work published in French, 1964).

Merleau-Ponty, M. (1992). *Sense and non-sense.* (Northwestern & P. Dreyfus, Trans.). Evanston, IL: Northwestern Press & Patricia Dreyfus. (Original work published in French, 1948).

Michael, D. G. (2011). Voice pedagogy: Dispelling vocal myths. Part 2: "Sing it off the chords!" *Journal of Singing, 7*(4), 417-421.

Miller, D. G. (2008). *Resonance in singing: Voice building through acoustic feedback.* Princeton: Inside View Press.

Miller, J. P. (2007). *The holistic curriculum.* Toronto: University of Toronto Press.

Miller, R. (1977). *English, French, German and Italian techniques of singing: A study in national tonal preferences and how they relate to functional efficiency.* Lanham, MD: Scarecrow Press.

Miller, R. (1986). *The structure of singing. System and art in vocal technique.* New York: Schirmer Books.

Miller, R. (1996). *On the art of singing.* Oxford: Oxford University Press.

Miller, R. (1997). *National schools of singing: English, French, German and Italian techniques of signing revisited.* Lanham, MD: Scarecrow Press.

Miller, R. (2003). (1) The unique teacher; (2) Holistic singing. *Journal of Singing, 59*(4), 317-318.

Miller, R. (2004). *Solutions for singers: Tools for performers and teachers.* New York: Oxford University Press.

Miller, R. (2008). *Securing baritone, bass-baritone, and bass voices*. New York: Oxford University Press.

Mogalakwe, M. (2006). The use of documentary research methods in social research. *African Sociological Review, 10*(1), 221-230.

Monahan, B. J. (1978). *The art of singing: A compendium of thoughts on singing published between 1777 and 1927*. Metuchen, NJ: Scarecrow Press.

Moran, D. (2000). *Introduction to phenomenology*. New York: Routledge.

Morgan, L. (2010). *Inside yourself: A new way to health based on the Alexander Technique*. (2nd ed.). London: Mouritz.

Morris, V. C. (1954). Existentialism and education. *Educational Theory, 4*(4), 247-258.

Morris, V. C. (1961). Existentialism and the education of the twentieth century man. *Educational Theory, 11*(1), 52-60.

Mortyakova, J. V. (2009). Existential piano teacher: The application of Jean-Paul Sartre's philosophy to piano instruction in a higher educational setting. Retrieved from ProQuest Digital Dissertations. (UMI 3358229)

Motherwell College (2020). Retrieved from http://www.motherwell.co.uk/courses/

Moustakas, C. (1994). *Phenomenological research methods*. Thousand Oaks, CA: Sage Publications.

National Center for Voice and Speech (2013). Retrieved from http://www.ncvs.org/ingo_bio.html

Naples, J. (1971). Existentialism and aesthetic education. *Music Educators Journal, 58*(3), 26-29.

Nayak, A. K., & Rao, V. K. (2008). *Educational psychology*. New Delhi: APH Publishing Corporation

Nelson, S., & Blades, E. (2005). Singing with your whole self: The Feldenkrais method and voice. *Journal of Singing, 62*(2), 145-157.

New England Conservatory (2020). Vocal Pedagogy. Retrieved from http://necmusic.edu/voice-opera

Noddings, N. (2007). *Philosophy of education*. Boulder, CO: Westview Press.

Northwestern University (2020). Vocal Lab. Retrieved from http://www.oto-hns.northwestern.edu/Voice/

Noudelmann, F. (2012). *The philosopher's touch: Sartre, Nietzsche, and Barthes at the piano*. (B. J. Reilly, Trans.). New York: Columbia University Press.

Oberlin College Conservatory (2020). Retrieved from http://new.oberlin.edu/conservatory/

Ohio State University (2020). Vocal Pedagogy. Retrieved from http://music.osu.edu/sites/music.osu.edu/files/MA-Vocal%20Pedagogy.pdf

Olivares, O., Peterson, G., & Hess, K. P. (2007). An existential-phenomenological framework for understanding leadership development experiences. *Leadership & Organization Development Journal, 28*(1), 76-91.

Osborne, H. (1991). Assessment and Stature. In R. Smith & A. Simpson (Eds.), *Aesthetics and arts education* (95-107). Chicago: University of Illinois Press.

Osborne, J. (1990). Some basic existential-phenomenological research methodology for counsellors. *Canadian Journal of Counselling, 24*(2), 79-91.

Otto Schoepfle Vocal Arts Center (2020). Retrieved from http://new.oberlin.edu/conservatory/departments/voice/vocal-arts-center/

Patenaude-Yarnelle, J. (2003). The private studio: A delicate balance: developing an individual approach to the new student. *Journal of Singing, 59*(3), 253-256.

Patenaude-Yarnelle, J. (2004). The most frequent technical problems found in young singers. *Journal of Singing, 60*(5), 491-495.

Patty, A. (1967). Existential teaching. *Educational Theory, 17*(4), 329-334.

Peterson, P. H. (2004). Devising an effective teacher training program for graduate assistants. *Journal of Singing, 61*(2), 155-159.

Princeton University (2020). Department of Music. Retrieved from http://www.princeton.edu/music/index.xml

Regan, P. (2012). Hans-Georg Gadamer's philosophical hermeneutics: Concepts of reading, understanding and interpretation. Meta: *Research in Hermeneutics, Phenomenology and Practical Philosophy, 4*(2), 280-303.

Reid, C. (1972). *The free voice: A guide to natural singing.* New York: Joseph Patelson Music House.

Richards, J. (2020). Holistic Singing. Retrieved from http://jesserichards.net/holisticsinging/index.htm

Riggs, S. (2007). Speech Level Singing™. Retrieved from http://www.sethriggs.com/seth-qa.html and http://www.sethriggs.com/index.html

Ristad, E. (1982). *A soprano on her head: Right-side-up reflections on life and other performances.* Moab, UT: Real People Press.

Robinson, P. (1973). Sartre on music. *The Journal of Aesthetics and Art Criticism, 31*(4), 451-457.

Rogers, C., & Freiberg, H. J. (1994). *Freedom to learn* (3rd ed.). New York, NY: Macmillan College.

Rogers, C. R. (1976). Carl Rogers and humanistic education. In C. H. Patterson (Ed.), *Foundations for a theory of instruction and educational psychology.* New York: Harper & Row.

Royans School of Vocal Science (2020). Retrieved from http://www.vocalscience.com/

Sadolin, C. (2000). *Complete vocal technique.* Copenhagen, Denmark: Shout Publishing.

Samoiloff, L. (1942). *The singer's handbook.* Philadelphia: Theodore Presser.

Sanford, S. A. (1995). A comparison of French and Italian singing in the seventeenth century. *Journal of Seventeen-Century Music, 1*(1).

Sartre, J. P. (1960). *Transcendence of the ego.* (F. Williams & R. Kirkpatrick, Trans.). New York: Hill and Wang.

Sartre, J. P. (1965). *Situations.* (B. Eisler, Trans.). New York: George Braziller.

Sartre, J. P. (1984). *Being and nothingness.* (H. E. Barnes, Trans.). New York: Washington Square Press.

Sartre, J. P. (1993). *Essays in existentialism.* W. Baskin (Ed.). New York: Kensington.

Sartre, J. P. (2001). *Jean-Paul Sartre: Basic writings.* S. Priest (Ed.). London: Routledge.

Sartre, J. P. (2007). *Existentialism is a humanism.* (C. Macomber, Trans.) New Haven: Yale University Press.

Sataloff, R. T. (1985) Vocal health. *Opera Digest*, Philadelphia Opera Company, Academy of Music, Philadelphia, Pennsylvania.

Sataloff, R., & Titze, I. (Eds.). (1991) *Vocal health and science. A compilation of articles from the NATS bulletin and the NATS journal.* Jacksonville, FL: National Association of Teachers of Singing.

Sataloff, R. T. (1998). *Vocal health and pedagogy: Science and assessment.* San Diego: Singular Publishing.

Scherer, R., Brewer, D., Colton, R., Rubin, L., Raphael, B., Miller, R., Moore, P. (1994). The integration of voice science, voice pathology, medicine, public speaking, acting, and singing. *Journal of Voice, 8*(4), 357-374.

Segall, W., & Wilson, A. V. (2004). *Introduction to education: teaching a diverse society.* Lanham, MD: Rowman and Littlefield.

Sell, K. (2005). *The disciplines of vocal pedagogy: Towards a holistic approach.* Burlington: Ashgate.

Shakespeare, W. (1910). *The art of singing*. Bryn Mawr, PA: Oliver Ditson.

Shenandoah University (2020). Vocal Pedagogy. Retrieved from http://www.su.edu/conservatory/MusicPedagogy.asp

Siegell, H. (2020). Holistic Voice NYC. Retrieved from http://holisticvoicenyc.com/index.php

Simonson, D. (2012). Recent research in singing. *Journal of Singing, 69* (1), 93-95.

Smith, B., & Smith, D. W. (1995). *The Cambridge companion to Husserl*. Cambridge: Cambridge University Press.

Smith, W. S., & Chipman, M. (2007). *The naked voice: A wholistic approach to singing*. New York: Oxford University Press.

Smithrim, K. (2003), Singing lessons: A hidden pedagogy. *Journal of the Canadian Association for Curriculum Studies, 1*(2), 53-62.

Somatic Voicework™ The LoVetri Method (2020). Retrieved from http://www.somaticvoicework.com/

Sounding Circles (2020). Holistic Voice Lessons. Retrieved from http://soundingcircles.com/page/holistic-voice-lessons

Speech Level Singing™ (2007). Retrieved from http://www.speechlevelsinging.com/slsmethod.html

Spiers, J. A. (2004). Tech tips: Using video management/analysis technology in qualitative research. *International Journal of Qualitative Methods, 3*(1), 1-8.

Stark, J. (1999). *Bel canto: A history of vocal pedagogy*. Toronto: University of Toronto Press.

Striny, D. (2007). *Head first. The language of the head voice: A concise study of learning to sing in the head voice*. Lanham, MD: Hamilton Books.

Striny, D. (2011). *Great singers. An endangered species: How to get back to Mother Nature*. Lanham, MD: Hamilton Books.

Suhanin, A. (2020). Holistic Voice Instructor. Retrieved from http://anitasuhanin.com/

Sundberg, J. (1977). The acoustics of the singing voice. *Scientific American, 236* (3), 82-91.

Sunnarborg, M. (2020). *Learning Solutions Magazine*. Retrieved from http://www.learningsolutionsmag.com/authors/75/michael-sunnarborg

Swift, A. (2006). *Political philosophy. A beginner's guide for students and politicians*. Cambridge: Polity Press.

Taylor, D. (1922). *The psychology of singing. A rational method of voice culture based on a scientific analysis of all systems, ancient and modern*. New York: MacMillan.

Teachey, J., Kahane, J., & Beckford, N. (1991). *Journal of Voice, 5*(1), 51-56.

Titze, I. (1994). *Principles of vocal production*. Englewood Cliffs, NJ: Prentice Hall.

Titze, I. (2011). Voice research and technology. *Journal of Singing, 68*(1), 49-50.

University of Central Florida (2020). Department of Theatre. Retrieved from http://theatre.cah.ucf.edu/

University of Central Oklahoma (2020). Department of Music. Retrieved from http://www.uco.edu/cfad/academics/music/index.asp http://acm.uco.edu/

University of Colorado (2020). Vocal Pedagogy. Retrieved from http://music.colorado.edu/departments/voice/areas-of-study/vocal-pedagogy/

University of Miami (2020). Vocal Pedagogy. Retrieved from http://www.miami.edu/frost/index.php/ vocal performance/degrees/

University of North Carolina (2020). Vocal Pedagogy. Retrieved from http://coaa.uncc.edu/Academics/Department-of-music/

University of North Texas (2020). Vocal Pedagogy. Retrieved from http://music.unt.edu/areas-of-study/detail/40

University of Texas, Austin (2020). Vocal Pedagogy. Retrieved fromhttp://music.utexas.edu/areas/details.aspx?id=11

University of Toronto (2020). Vocal Pedagogy. Retrieved from http://www.music.utoronto.ca/Page2418.aspx

van Manen, M. (1984). Practicing phenomenological writing. *Phenomenology + Pedagogy, 2*(1), 36-69.

van Manen, M. (1990). *Researching lived experience: Human science for an action sensitive pedagogy*. Albany, NY: State University of New York Press.

van Manen, M. (1991). *The tact of teaching: The meaning of pedagogical thoughtfulness*. Albany, NY: The State University of New York Press.

van Manen, M. (2007). Phenomenology of practice. *Phenomenology & Practice, 1*(1), 11-30.

Vennard, W. (1967). *Singing. The mechanism and the technic*. New York: Carl Fischer.

Vocal Science™ Method (2020). Retrieved from http://www.vocalscience.com/

Wakefield, G. (2003). Vocal pedagogy and pedagogical voices. Proceedings of the 2003 International Conference on Auditory Display.

Ware, C. (1998). *Basics of vocal pedagogy: The foundations and process of singing*. New York: McGraw-Hill.

Webber, J. (2006). Sartre's theory of character. *European Journal of Philosophy, 14*(1), 94-116.

Weber, S. (1986). The nature of interviewing. *Phenomenology + Pedagogy, 4*(2), 65-72.

Webley, L. (2010). Qualitative approaches to empirical legal research. In P. Cane & H. Kritzer (Eds.), The *Oxford handbook of empirical legal research* (926-950). Oxford: Oxford University Press.

Webster, S. (2002). Existentialism: Providing an ideal framework for educational research in times of uncertainty ®, *in AARE 2002: Problematic* futures: educational research in an era of uncertainty; AARE 2002 conference papers, Australian Association for Research in Education, Coldstream, Vic. pp. 1-15. Retrieved from http://hdl.handle.net/10536/DRO/DU:30033908

Wei, C. T. (2006). Role and efficacy of verbal imagery in teaching: Case study and computer analysis. Retrieved from ProQuest Digital Dissertations. (UMI 3251829)

Westfall, K. G. (2012). A model of an effective approach to studio voice at the undergraduate level: The vocal method of Dr. Raquel Cortina. Retrieved from ProQuest Digital Dissertations. (UMI 3514730)

Westminster Choir College (2020). Vocal Pedagogy. Retrieved from http://www.rider.edu/wcc/academics/graduate-programs/master-music-voice-pedagogy-and-performance#pedagogy

Whitlock, W. (1975). *Profiles in vocal pedagogy: A textbook for singing teachers.* Ann Arbor, MI: Clifton Press.

Woodruff, N. (2011). Contemporary commercial voice pedagogy applied to the choral ensemble: An interview with Jeannette LoVetri. *Choral Journal, 52*(5), 41-52.

Wurgler, P. S. (1997). Voice pedagogy: The process of teaching the art of singing. *Journal of Singing, 53*(5), 3-8.

Yanagisawa, E., Estill, J., Kmucha, S., & Leder, S. (1989). The contribution of aryepiglottic constriction to "ringing" voice quality. *Journal of Voice, 3*(4), 342-35.

www.ingramcontent.com/pod-product-compliance
Lightning Source LLC
Chambersburg PA
CBHW062027290426
44108CB00025B/2805